MW01200298

CONCERNING
FREQUENT COMMUNION
OF THE IMMACULATE MYSTERIES OF CHRIST

THE WORKS
OF SAINT NIKODEMOS
THE HAGIORITE

Detail of the Mystical Supper, Katholicon, Holy Monastery of Stavronikita, Mount Athos.

CONCERNING
FREQUENT COMMUNION
OF THE IMMACULATE MYSTERIES OF CHRIST

by our Righteous God-bearing Father
Nikodemos the Hagiorite

INCLUDING
A thorough explanation of the Lord's Prayer,
an apology for frequent communion, answers to
objections and clarifications of misconceptions,
and two appendices on the Divine Eucharist

Translated by Fr. George Dokos

Uncut Mountain Press

CONCERNING FREQUENT COMMUNION OF THE IMMACULATE MYSTERIES OF CHRIST

Second Edition

Copyright © 2006, 2023
by Uncut Mountain Press

All rights reserved under International and Pan-American Copyright Conventions. Designed and published by Uncut Mountain Press.

uncutmountainpress.com

This translation has been made from the Greek text of the first edition published by Nektarios Panagopoulos (Athens, 2001).

Front Cover Photograph: Portable icon from the Holy Monastery of the Paraclete, Oropos, Greece.

Cover Artwork: George Weis

Scriptural quotations are primarily taken from the King James Version. The translator to better reflect the original Greek text has emended some quotations. All citations of the Psalms are taken from The Psalter Acording to the Seventy, translated from the Septuagint Version of the Old Testament by the Holy Transfiguration Monastery, Brookline, MA.

Concerning Frequent Communion of the Immaculate Mysteries of Christ—2nd ed.
Nikodemos the Hagiorite, Saint, 1749-1809
Translated and annotated by George Dokos.

ISBN: 978-1-63941-029-3

I. Christianity—Eastern Orthodox Spirituality
II. Christianity—Spiritual Instruction

Verily, verily, I say unto you,
Except ye eat the flesh of the Son of man,
and drink His blood, ye have no life in you.
Whoso eateth My flesh, and drinketh My blood,
hath eternal life; and I will raise him up at the last day.
For My flesh is meat indeed, and My blood is drink indeed.
He that eateth My flesh, and drinketh My blood,
dwelleth in Me, and I in him.

John 6:53–56

Ἀφιεροῦται πᾶσι τοῖς μυσταγωγοῖς,
Τῆς ἡμῶν Ἐκκλησίας Ἀποστολικῆς,
Οἷς ἀνήχασιν ἡμᾶς εἰς τοὺς οὐρανούς,
Καὶ εἰς τὰ βαθέα μυστήρια Θεοῦ.

Saint Nikodemos the Hagiorite, Katholikon, Annunciation Monastery, Patmos.

APOLYTIKION

Tone 3. Awed by the beauty.

Adorned wast thou O Father* by the grace of wisdom*
inspired thou appeared as* a trumpet of the Spirit*
and as a teacher of virtues* Nikodemos who speaks of God*
for to all hast thou offered* teachings of salvation*
and purity of life* pouring forth enlightenment*
by the richness of thy virtuous writings*
through which as light thou hast illumined the world.

TABLE OF CONTENTS

PART TWO
CONCERNING FREQUENT COMMUNION

PART THREE
OBJECTIONS - CLARIFICATIONS

APPENDIX A
ON WHAT THE MYSTERY OF THE DIVINE EUCHARIST REPRESENTS

APPENDIX B
CONCERNING THE MYSTERY OF THE DIVINE EUCHARIST

PREFACE

When the present book was first published by St. Nikodemos the Hagiorite and St. Makarios Notaras, it had as its objective to elevate the spiritual life of Christians. At the same time, it was also a response to a certain attitude which had become the status quo, and an ideology, and which deterred Christians from their frequent participation in the divine communion of the immaculate Mysteries.

This matter was one of the basic subjects with which the so-called Philokalic movement of the eighteenth century was concerned. St. Nikodemos and St. Makarios are the most important representatives of the Philokalic movement, a movement of spiritual renewal within the Church. The period of Turkish oppression (1453–1821) had brought the spiritual life of the Christians of that time into decline. The most fundamental objectives of the movement were the observance of the sacred Canons, frequent participation in divine Communion, a return to the Fathers, the practice of noetic prayer, and the renewal of monasticism.

Even today we are living the reverberations of this movement of Fathers, most of whom have been acknowledged as Saints. And this is what sets it apart from the activity of contemporary "modernists," who resort to innovations not founded upon the tradition of the Saints. The Saints are bearers of tradition, and it is in them that we place our trust when it comes to matters of the Church. They are those who are instructed and led by the Holy Spirit, expressing the truth of the Faith in every era. Certainly, every era requires its own mode of expression, but "the truth of he Lord abideth for ever" (Ps. 116:2).

Unfortunately, we can say that the status quo attitude was not overturned. Few were influenced by the Philokalic movement. The fruit of that struggle mainly appeared at the end of the nineteenth century and in the twentieth century. And only a portion of the people today can be characterized as being a part of the liturgical life of the Church, attending services, going to confession, and struggling in the spiritual life. Most of today's people are far from the Cup of life, and continue to offer the same justifications to excuse this lapse. Most Christians who do go to Church, but do not think it necessary to commune of the body and blood of Christ, are of the same attitude.

We live in a time of decline in ecclesiastical life. From the moment when most churchgoers wittingly and stubbornly abstain from divine Communion, we live in an ecclesiastical decline, for growth or decline is indicated by the participation of the faithful in this Mystery.

One time in a certain homily I told the people, "If you were to ask us priests when we will be pleased with our pastoral work, we would reply: 'Only when we reach the point that every Sunday during the Divine Liturgy all of the Christians have prepared themselves and receive Communion, will we say that we are pleased with our pastoral work.'"

Academic theology systematically ignored, and largely still ignores, the Fathers of the Philokalic movement. As theology students, we never heard anything from a single one of our professors at the Theological School about this movement or about St. Nikodemos the Hagiorite. Now, finally, some interest has begun to appear, and this gives us hope. If only the academic theological world would also be irrigated by their theology, and if only the shepherds would offer the solid food of the Saints of the Philokalia to the spiritually needy.

Because of the prevailing condition we have described, Saints Nikodemos and Makarios's book, *Concerning Frequent Communion*, is highly relevant. This translation and publication in the English language will afford the faithful the ability to come into contact with the treasures of the Orthodox Faith and to be fed by the works of the Fathers of the Philokalia.

We hope that the publication of such books will help in overcoming our ecclesiastical decline.

Archimandrite Chrysostom Maidones
Chancellor and Homilist
Sacred Metropolis of Hierissos

July 14, 2006
The Commemoration of St Nikodemos the Hagiorite

The Kollyvades Fathers
Saint Nikodemos the Hagiorite,
Saint Athanasios of Paros, Saint Makarios of Corinth

A BRIEF HISTORY OF THE PRESENT BOOK [1]

The first edition of this work had the following title: "A handbook, by an anonymous author, demonstrating that Christians must partake of the divine Mysteries more frequently. Now published for the first time and made possible at the expense of the most honorable and devout Mr. Demetrios Proskynetos of Drysta. Published in Venice, 1777, by Nicholas Glykes of Ioannina. Con Licenza de 'Superiori."

It is considered as certain that the author hidden beneath the work's anonymity is St. Makarios Notaras. The biographer of this divine Father, St. Athanasios Parios, who also attributes the work's authorship to Makarios, offers the following brief analysis of it: "This work appears to contain nothing other than sayings from the Gospels, Apostles, Canons (Apostolic and Conciliar), and the divine Fathers, all explained in our popular dialect. They are all in accord and have the same conclusion, teaching that frequent reception of the divine Mysteries is good, holy, and salvific. Wherefore, this book is holy and lawful and canonical, because, as we said, it contains nothing other than scriptural, canonical, and patristic sayings, interpreted and explained in the vernacular without a single distortion or mistake, as everyone can see."[2]

---

1 From Anthony N. Charokopos's *Ho Hagios Makarios ho Notaras, Metropolites Korinthou (1731–1805)* [*St. Makarios Notaras, Metropolitan of Corinth (1731–1805)*] (Athens: 2001), 182–188.

2 Athanasios Parios, *Bios kai Politeia tou hosiou kai theophorou patros Makariou, Archiepiskopou*

However, the work met with great resistance: "Even with all this," continues the biographer, "evil waxed mightily against it. When a certain evil-minded monk of the Holy Mountain received the book into his hands, thinking it was the work of Neophytos, he sent it via Thessaloniki to the Great Church in Constantinople, having a certain friend of his write as many bad things against it as he could. Patriarch Prokopios the Peloponnesian (1785–1789), who had then ascended the Patriarchal Throne from Smyrna, based solely on the accusations and criticisms regarding the book, was startled and without delay condemned the work synodically as unlawful and scandalous, meting out the severest penances to those who would dare read it. The brethren of Mt. Athos, through another individual, tried to repeal the condemnation of the book by means of a counter-decision of the Church, but they were unsuccessful. So the wrong remained uncorrected."[3]

However, via another reliable source, which published the patriarchal text,[4] we are informed that the patriarch at that time was not Prokopios from Smyrna as the biographer writes, but Gabriel IV (1780–1785). This source cites a condemnation also by Prokopios, without citing the document, deriving its information from the biographer.[5] We do not know if there was actually a second condemnation of the book. Perhaps the biographer was misled.

Here we add the entire lengthy patriarchal text:[6]

Korinthou tou Notara [*Life and Conduct of the Righteous and Godbearing Father Makarios Notaras, Archbishop of Corinth*], in *Neon Chiakon Leimonarion*, 7th Edition, (Chios: 1992), 241.

3 Ibid. See also Tzoga, *He peri mnemosynon eris en Hagio Orei kata ton 18 aiona* [*The Controversy on the Holy Mountain During the 18th Century Concerning Memorial Services*] (Thessaloniki: 1969), 120–130.

4 Manuel J. Gedeon, *Kanonikai Diataxeis: Epistolai, Lyseis, Thespismata, ton hagiotaton Patriarchon Konstantinoupoleos. Apo Gregoriou tou Theologou mechri Dionysiou tou apo Adrianoupoleos* [*Canonical Constitutions: Epistles, Solutions, Ordinances, of the Most-holy Patriarchs of Constantinople. From Gregory the Theologian to Dionysios of Adrianoupolis*], supplement to "Ekklesiastikes Aletheias," vol. 1 (Constantinople: 1888), 269–272.

5 Ibid., 272.

6 Ibid., 269–272.

Gabriel, by the mercy of God Archbishop of Constantinople and New Rome and Ecumenical Patriarch.

Most-reverend Superintendents of the Community, former and current Abbots of our sacred and venerable Patriarchal and Stavropegic Monasteries of the Most-holy Mountain of Athos, and the rest of the Fathers dwelling in the monasteries, cells and sketes, our beloved children in the Lord: grace be with you and peace from God. To slip and fall into sins is terrible and damaging to the soul. But even more terrible, if not the most damaging, is when the fallen one does not want to get up and when the sinner does not repent or listen to advice unto his correction. The passions of sin are healed by the medicines of penitence and abstinence, but where these medicines are unable to have their effect, no hope of life remains. Therefore, those who are unrepentant are more wicked than those who are sinful and thus worthy of greater punishment and condemnation, in the same degree as incurable diseases are worse than curable ones. You, however, will not behave in such a manner, but you will rather amend your ways and obey the Great and Holy Church of Christ, and desist henceforth from your unreasonable disputes and quarrels. For there appeared before our Synod an anonymous book, Concerning Sacred Communion, already published and in print, and a letter stamped with the seal of your Community stating that on account of this book many quarrels and disputes have arisen and developed there. Some people accept it and say that it is necessary to partake of the immaculate Mysteries of Christ every day, in accordance with the thesis of the book; but other people oppose it and assert that one must first prepare many days beforehand through confession, self-control, and appropriate repentance, and then approach sacred Communion.

These things, then, are contained in the letter of your Community. The book, being read and inspected, appeared at the first to be flawed and full of misunderstandings and absurdities, and then later as also contrary to the ecclesiastical good order and practice which has always been in effect. From time immemorial our Holy and blameless Church has never given the task of examining and adjudicating regarding the dogmas and sacred Mysteries to just

anyone, or to any single person; but, rather, She knows that this is
the work of a complete and supremely perfect council. And those
things that have been approved and declared by the Church to be
correct are given to the faithful for their use, as being beneficial
to the soul. But the others are rightly disapproved and rejected as
being erroneous and damaging to the soul, horrible and hateful to
Christians, even if there is something correct in them. Many times
there have been men who have insidiously attempted to penetrate
and corrupt correct and healthy things of our blameless Church,
at the suggestion of the devil and under the pretense of piety and
virtue. The writer of this little book, shamelessly and very boldly,
with utter arrogance, went too far and took matters into his own
hands, setting himself against ancient ecclesiastical good order
and custom. And though he displayed the work to all, the author
himself hid away in an unknown place and did not even place his
own name on it. For, being conscious of the greatness of his sin and
fearing chastisement and punishment, he concealed himself, in this
way safely lying in wait, and then out of nowhere treacherously
ambushing and springing upon the naive and the simple. For these
reasons, then, this anonymous little book was deemed altogether
outrageous and worthy of rejection, as incorrect and causing
scandals, and also as being contrary to ancient ecclesiastical good
order.

Concerning the proper time for partaking of the divine and
immaculate Mysteries, it is confessed [by us] that it is beneficial to
receive Communion more frequently, if only it is done worthily. For
our blameless faith knows that the worthy reception of Communion
is necessary and among those things without which we cannot live.
The proper time to receive Communion, as the great Father of the
Church the sacred Chrysostom says, is not at the occasion of a Feast
and celebration [as such], but when we have a pure conscience and
a life free of evil deeds. And again, continuing, the same Father
says: "Whenever you intend to partake of this Holy Offering, purify
yourself many days beforehand through repentance and prayer and
almsgiving, through occupying yourself with spiritual things, and

by not returning to your own vomit as does the dog."[7] Therefore, according to the sacred Chrysostom and the divine Apostle, "Let a man examine himself, and so let him eat of the bread, and drink of the cup" (1 Cor. 11:28). So, that the dissension, quarreling, the arrogant and unseasonable dispute caused by the aforementioned book shall cease, through the present letter, and with the agreement of the All-holy former Patriarchs of Constantinople, Ioannikios and Theodosios, and of His Beatitude and Holiness Patriarch Abramios, our dear and beloved brothers and concelebrants in the Holy Spirit, we, with the rest of our brethren and highly-honored and holy hierarchs, make a synodical declaration. We order all of you, as many as possess the aforementioned anonymous book concerning Communion, to immediately reject it and throw it away as being flawed and unlawful, without any of you daring to take it into his hands and read it—and so the exchange of words and disputes shall come to an end. Furthermore: Let nobody dare to write or say anything concerning matters that are not his concern; but, rather, all of you are to live and conduct yourselves in peace and concord in stillness, according to your profession, trusting in our synodical order and command. And may all those acting in this fashion as directed be forgiven and blessed by God the Lord Almighty and absolved and freed from the previously published penalties. However, whoever among you dares to write or speak from now on concerning these issues and disturbs the stillness of the Fathers in these places, as self-willed and disobedient to our patriarchal and synodical commands and as a rebel and lover of disturbance and causer of scandals, let him be anathematized, etc. (the usual curses). Let it be so by decree.

1785. In the month of April. Third Indiction.

Former Patriarch of Constantinople Ioannikios co-decrees.

Abramios of Jerusalem co-decrees. Samuel of Ephesus. Methodios of Herakleia. Agapios of Kylikos. Gerasimos of Nikomedeia. Parthenios of Chalcedon. Ananias of Derkos. Matthew of Serres. Gregory of Drama. Meletios of Nauploion.

---

7 *De Beato Philogonio* 4, PG 48, 755.

Later, however, the book was vindicated, as is apparent from the epistle of Patriarch Neophytos VII (1789–1798 and 1798–1801) written between the years 1789–1794 to the most-holy Father, Makarios. This epistle of the patriarch "to the former Metropolitan of Corinth," published by the biographer of the illustrious hierarch,[8] reads as follows:

Most-sacred former Metropolitan of Corinth Makarios, beloved in the Spirit and concelebrant with our Mediocrity, grace be with your arch-priesthood and peace from God. Concerning the written work of your arch-priesthood, the book concerning frequent sacred Communion, which you published in print, we make known to you that it was examined synodically, carefully inspected, and approved and confirmed as ecclesiastically lawful and as containing no impediment as to its use. However, those who worthily desire to frequently partake of the immaculate and dread Mysteries must do so through repentance and true confession. And when they frequently commune with this lawful and God-pleasing preparation, frequent communion is very lawful and beneficial to the soul and salvific. Therefore, your book was synodically declared beneficial and salvific, since it demonstrates this lawful manner of receiving Communion, and those wishing to buy it may read it unhindered, and they may receive Communion with the fear of God, lawfully and canonically, with the guidance and satisfaction [of the assigned spiritual rule] of each person's Spiritual Father. These are worthy to receive frequently. However, because a suspicion has grown that an ecclesiastical excommunication has been pronounced condemning your written work, and therefore, in order to respect the "excommunication," pious Christians do not read it, we write in this present letter and declare through the All-holy and Officiating Spirit the dissolution of these ecclesiastical bonds and penalties: "All those Christians desiring to read your synodically examined written work, that is, your book concerning frequent Communion, are forgiven and blessed by God the Lord Almighty, being no longer constrained by the ecclesiastical penalties and having no curses; they

---

8 Parios, 241–242. See also Papoulides, 57.

even have the prayers and blessings of all the Saints and holy people and God-bearing Fathers of the Church through all the centuries. Therefore, Your Sacredness, dismiss every mistrust and suspicion about your work, since you will receive reward from God for your written work, being as it is beneficial to the soul, and may His grace be with you."

Before the book's acquittal, the divine Makarios, on account of the manifest resistance against it, gave the work over to St. Nikodemos the Hagiorite for it to be worked on further and revised. So the work was republished after six years in 1783 by St. Nikodemos with the title: "A book most profitable to the soul concerning frequent Communion of the immaculate Mysteries of Christ. Now published for the first time unto the common benefit of Orthodox Christians. Published in Venice, 1783, by Anthony Bertoli. Con Licenza de 'Superiori e Rrivilegio."[9] This book also contains an explanation of the Lord's Prayer, which is absent from the 1777 edition. Evidently, this work too was published anonymously, but it is considered certain that Nikodemos the Hagiorite is its author, the one responsible for the revision, the enriching amendments, and the additions to the text of the 1777 edition.[10]

In that we wish to be as thorough as possible, we note that, concerning the authorship of the work, or rather, of the works— that is, of the 1777 edition and of the 1783 edition—there has arisen a literary controversy.[11] We will not proceed here with an analysis of the controversy, but simply note in brief the opinions of the researchers.

Most attribute the 1777 edition to Makarios of Corinth (L. Petit, S. Makres, K. Doukakes, J. Konstantinides, N. Zacharopoulos,

---

9 Theokletos Dionysiates, *Hagios Nikodemos ho Hagiorites: Ho bios kai ta erga tou (1749–1809)* [*St. Nikodemos the Hagiorite: His Life and Works (1749–1809)*], (Athens: 1959), 110 ff.

10 For an analysis see: *Hierod. Neophytou Kausokalybitou, Peri tes sychnes Metalepseos, Eisagoge – Keimenon (anekdoton) – Scholia* [*Hierodeacon Neophytos Kavsokalyvites, Concerning Frequent Communion, Introduction – Text (unpublished) – Scholia*], Hieromonk Theodoret the Hagiorite, 2nd ed. (Athens: 1992), 7 ff. where there is also an analytical bibliography – references.

11 Dionysiates, 110. This viewpoint is contested by K. K. Papoulides (133, n93).

and G. Berites), and the reworked 1783 edition to Nikodemos the
Hagiorite in collaboration with the sacred Makarios (basically all
of the aforementioned), or only to Nikodemos (M. Gedeon, who
also presented a modified viewpoint).[12] Others (H. Hodges and
others) maintain that the 1783 edition belongs entirely to Makarios
of Corinth. Theokletos Dionysiates attributes the 1777 edition
to Neophytos Kavsokalyvites.[13] This opinion is mainly supported

---

12 Translator's note: The early biographers of St. Nikodemos, such as Euthymios (1812)
and Onouphrios Ivirites (1819), and the more recent biographers, such as Gerasimos
Mikragiannanites (1955) and Theokletos Dionysiates (1959), all agree that St. Nikodemos
received the book in its original form from St. Makarios (whoever its original author might
have been), but then edited, corrected, and expanded it. Furthermore, St. Nikodemos
himself witnesses to the fact that he wrote it, defending it as his own in the *Apologia* he
wrote almost thirty years later (*Homologia Pisteos* [*Confession of Faith*], written in 1807, but
published posthumously at Venice in 1819). The final form as we have received it is
undoubtedly from the pen of St. Nikodemos. Nevertheless, it is a definite product of the
"school" of the *Kollyvades*, as are all the works of St. Nikodemos. He was not a freelance
writer expressing his private opinion, but always received assignments from holy men such
as St. Makarios, writing everything with a blessing. It is also worth noting here what Dr.
George Bebis writes concerning this work:

> The book was not authored originally by St. Nicodemos himself. Father Theokletos
> Dionysiatis has expressed the opinion that it came from the pen of the Hagiorite monk
> Neophytos, who was one of the protagonists of the *Kollyvades*. Recently, the Hagiorite
> monk Theodore has discovered the original manuscript of Neophytos in the library of
> the Academy of Bucharest, Roumania, dated in 1772, as well as the first printed edition
> made in the more popular language, which was edited in 1777. Father Theodore has
> proved beyond any doubt that St. Nicodemos' edition in 1783 was based on Neophytos'
> work. St. Macarios encouraged his friend to undergo a revision of this splendid book,
> and St. Nicodemos revised, enlarged, and enriched Neophytos' original work to such
> an extent that it may almost be considered a new book. St. Nicodemos extended the
> original 173 pages to 343,. He wrote two introductions, and divided the book into
> three parts. In the first part, in nine chapters, he analyzes and interprets the Lord's
> Prayer (not found in Neophytos' book); in the second part, he speaks about the need
> for frequent holy Communion; and, in the third part, in the form of questions and
> answers, he refutes the arguments of his opponents that frequent holy Communion is
> not proper and necessary. (*Nicodemos of the Holy Mountain: A Handbook of Spiritual Counsel*
> [New York: Paulist Press, CWS, 1989], 24–25)

13 *Hierod. Neophytou Kausokalybitou, Peri tes sychnes Metalepseos, Eisagoge − Keimenon (anekdoton)
− Scholia* [*Hierodeacon Neophytos Kavsokalyvites, Concerning Frequent Communion, Introduction − Text*

by Hieromonk Theodoret the Hagiorite, who also published Neophytos' original work, "as preserved until now in codices no. 988, 225a–261b and no. 192, 19a–60b of the Academy of Bucharest"[14] (1st ed., 1975; 2nd ed., 1992). A work by Neophytos Kavsokalyvites concerning frequent Communion of the immaculate Mysteries was reportedly published in 1766 (A. Demetrakopoulos and C. Patrineles), but according to Theodoret the Hagiorite, this has not been proven as of yet.[15] And S. Papadopoulos speaks of two books, one by Neopytos Kavsokalyvites, which was composed in 1772 and published, as is verified by Hieromonk Theodoret, and the other of St. Makarios.

(unpublished) – *Scholia*], Hieromonk Theodoret the Hagiorite, 2nd Edition (Athens: 1992).

14 Ibid., 10. For the opinion of C. Patrineles and the others mentioned above, see *Ekdotikes Athenon, Historia tou Hellenikou Ethnous* [*Athens Editorial, History of the Greek Nation*], vol. 11, 132.

15 Papoulides, 59–60. See also the sacred service of our Holy and Godbearing Father Christodoulos the Wonderworker, 5th ed. (Athens: 1957), 5.

The Saints of the Islands of Paros and Naxos

*(L–R) Saint Athanasios of Paros, Saint Nicolas Planas, Saint Theoktiste,
Saint Nikodemos the Hagiorite and Saint Philotheos Zervakos.*

ABBREVIATIONS

ACW	Ancient Christian Writers.
ANF	Anti-Nicene Fathers.
CSCO	Corpus Scriptorum Christianorum Orientalium.
CWS	The Classics of Western Spirituality.
FC	Fathers of the Church.
GrPhilokalia	Philokalia of the Sacred Neptic Fathers, ed. St. Nikodemos the Hagiorite and St. Makarios Notaras, Venice, 1782.
NPNF	Nicene and Post-Nicene Fathers.
PG	Patrologia Graeca.
The Philokalia	The Philokalia: The Complete Text, trans. and ed. G. E. H. Palmer, P. Sherrard, K. Ware, London and Boston, 1979 (volume 1), 1981 (volume 2), 1984 (volume 3), 1995 (volume 4).
PL	Patrologia Latina.
ST	Studi e Testi.
SC	Sources Chrétiennes, Paris.

The Crucifixion with Scenes from the Gospel, 14th c., Monastery of St. Catherine, Mount Sinai.

"For even Christ our passover is sacrificed for us..."

1 Cor. 5:7

CONCERNING
FREQUENT COMMUNION
OF THE IMMACULATE MYSTERIES OF CHRIST

Mystical Supper, Katholicon, Holy Monastery of Stavronikita, Mount Athos.

And as they were eating, Jesus took bread, and blessed it, and brake it, and gave it to the disciples, and said, Take, eat; this is my body. And he took the cup, and gave thanks, and gave it to them, saying, Drink ye all of it; For this is my blood of the new testament, which is shed for many for the remission of sins. Matt. 26:26-28

PROLOGUE

God, because He is by nature good, out of His great goodness willed to create all visible and invisible creatures out of nonbeing[16] so that they might also enjoy His goodness and rejoice with Him, which creatures He established by His Son and Word and perfected by His life-creating Spirit.[17] Then, from the visible and invisible world He also created man according to His very image, so that he might also become according to His likeness.[18] The body He fashioned by His own hands from the four elements, namely, from earth, air, water, and fire; and the rational soul He created through His own in-breathing.[19] "In the image" [kat' eikona] means that, just as God is Intellect [Nous] and rules everything and is able to do anything He wills, so also is the soul noetic [noeros] and rules over all the visible creatures and is free to do anything it wills. "In the likeness" [kath' homoisin] means that just as God has all the virtues by nature, so also man, acquiring the virtues by grace, becomes like God through the faculty of his free will.

God endowed man with ten senses, five of the soul and five of the body. The senses of the body are sight, hearing, smell, taste, and touch. Those of the soul are intellect, reason, judgment, imagination, and consciousness.[20] The soul also has three aspects:

---

16 Cf. Gen. 1:1; 2 Macc. 7:28.

17 Cf. Ps. 32:6.

18 Cf. Gen. 1:26.

19 Cf. Gen. 2:6–7.

20 Cf. Niketas Stethatos, *On the Practice of the Virtues* 10, *Philokalia of the Sacred Neptic Fathers* (Venice: 1782), 787 (henceforth referred to as *GrPhilokalia*); *The Philokalia:*

the intelligent aspect, the incensive aspect, and the appetitive aspect. The intellect was placed in the soul by God like an eye and like a king, encircled by the four general and universal virtues, namely, prudence, courage, restraint, and righteousness, in order that the intellect, by these four virtues, might rule the whole man. These virtues are begotten by the three aspects of the soul: from the rational aspect is begotten prudence and righteousness, from the incensive aspect is begotten courage, and from the appetitive aspect is begotten restraint. And the body is constituted from four parts, that is, from the four elements, and is like a second material world, while the soul has three aspects, as we said, signifying the Holy Trinity. With its intelligent aspect the soul thinks upon those good things that are beneficial to it. With its incensive aspect the soul becomes wrathful against the demons and the passions and stands against them. And with its appetitive aspect the soul loves God, Who is truly the Beloved, and, likewise, loves virtue and man who is in the image of God.

After God formed man and adorned him with such endowments, He then also planted Paradise in Eden, in the east, and placed man therein, in order that he might till and keep it.[21] God also gave man a commandment[22] that, if he chose to keep it, would make him immortal and a god by grace, eating of the tree of life. (For there were three types of trees in Paradise: some were for Adam that he might simply live, some were for him that he might live well, and still others were for him that he might live both well and forever.) But O, what disaster! On account of the devil's envy[23] pitiable man was beguiled and he disobeyed the divine commandment, and on account of this he was banished from that blessed life.[24] But God, again showing His philanthropy, did not alter His original plan for man, but waited until a chosen and worthy vessel would be born, one

---

The Complete Text, vol. 4 (London: Faber and Faber, 1995), 81 (henceforth referred to as *The Philokalia*).

21 Cf. Gen. 2:8, 15.

22 Cf. Gen. 2:16.

23 Cf. Wis. 2:24.

24 Cf. Gen. 3:1–24.

that would serve this exalted and great plan. So when she who was foreordained before the ages and chosen above all generations was born—I mean the Ever-virgin and Theotokos Mary—the Creator of all yearned for and loved the beauty of her virginity and her purity,[25] and so He bowed the heavens[26] and descended like gentle rain into her ever-virginal womb. And remaining God without change, He took on flesh and became perfect man,[27] by the good pleasure of the Father and the co-operation of the Holy Spirit.[28] And the Son and Word of God, sweet Jesus Christ our Lord, became a mediator between God and man[29] in order to show to him the Father,[30] Whom man did not know,[31] and in order to offer him to the Father through the Holy Spirit[32] and to reconcile him to the Father, putting to death the enmity between God and man by His own passion[33] and by His heavenly teachings and divine works. In brief, through His entire incarnate and dread economy He granted us such lofty and great gifts, and gave us so many heavenly and supranatural blessings, that it is impossible for any human mind or tongue to relate them one by one. And in addition to all the other things He left us in this present life as a fatherly inheritance and inexhaustible treasure, are the seven Holy and august Mysteries [Sacraments] of the Church, namely, Baptism, Myron [Chrismation], Communion, the Priesthood, Marriage, Repentance [or Confession], and Holy Oil [Unction], so that we may use them as the spiritual and chiefly necessary means for the healing and salvation of our souls. Of these seven, the most necessary and soul-saving are Holy Baptism and the Holy Communion of the body and blood of our Lord Jesus Christ,

---

25 Cf. Ps. 44:12.

26 Cf. Ps. 143:5.

27 Cf. Jn. 1:14.

28 Cf. Lk. 1:35.

29 Cf. 1 Tim. 2:5.

30 Cf. Jn. 14:9.

31 Cf. Jn. 7:28.

32 Cf. Heb. 9:14.

33 Cf. Eph. 2:16.

just as the sacred Dionysios the Areopagite[34] and many other divine teachers write.[35]

In the present book, our aim is not to speak about the other five Mysteries, [nor even about Baptism,] but only about the Mystery of divine Communion. And we will not even occupy ourselves with all of the aspects of this Mystery, but only with one aspect. That is to say, we will not concern ourselves here with the visible aspects of the performance and rite of the Mystery and how it is to be celebrated (which things the divine Dionysios calls symbolic icons[36]). Neither will we occupy ourselves with the interpretation and noetic contemplation of each sacred movement. And neither will we be concerned with the mediation which this Mystery accomplishes between the living and the dead and God. We will only be concerned here with the use of this Mystery and with its reception, in which only the living faithful participate. To be more clear, we will demonstrate from the Scriptures and from the Fathers that it is necessary for all of us living faithful and Orthodox Christians to receive the body and blood of the Lord frequently (as many, that is, who have not been placed under a rule not to receive Communion by their Spiritual Father), and that frequent Communion greatly benefits our souls and bodies; while, on the contrary, its infrequent or leisurely reception brings us great harm and destruction. Additionally, we will respond to the objections raised by those who are opposed to this.

However, because communicants must prepare themselves to receive through contrition, confession, and satisfaction [that is,

---

34 See *De Ecclesiastica Hierarchia*, chs. 2 and 3 (PG 3, 392A–404D and 424B–445C); *Pseudo-Dionysius: The Complete Works* (New York: Paulist Press, CWS, 1987), 200–224.

35 Translator's note: In his *Exomologetarion*, however, St. Nikodemos does state that the Mystery of Holy Confession and Repentance "is a bath which is a second baptism for penitents, more laborious than the first baptism, and just as necessary for salvation as the first baptism" (Athens: Panagopoulos, 2002), 196; trans. *Exomologetarion: A Manual of Confession* (Thessaloniki: Uncut Mountain Press, 2006), 302. Look also ahead to ch. 6 of Part One of the present work.

36 Cf. *De Ecclesiastica Hierarchia* 3.1.1, PG 3, 428A–428B; *Pseudo-Dionysius: The Complete Works*, 211–212.

the fulfilling of their ascetical rule, or kanon],[37] and through other prayers and compunctionate readings, and seeing that the sacred prayer which our Lord handed down, namely, the "Our Father," contains so many compunctionate words and meanings fitting for those who will commune, we thought it best to place an explanation of the Lord's Prayer at the beginning of the book. This is so that it might serve as a most appropriate preparation, in addition to the other preparations, for those desiring to commune; and for many other reasons as well, especially the following three:

Firstly, through this prayer, those planning to commune ask God the Father to give them the superessential [epiousios] bread, which is the body of the Lord. Secondly, with this prayer, they forgive all of the debts and trespasses of their brothers, thus purifying their heart of rancor and of any resentful feelings, which is a necessary preparation for Communion according to the word of the Lord: "Therefore if thou bring thy gift to the altar, and there rememberest that thy brother hath ought against thee; leave there thy gift before the altar, and go thy way; first be reconciled to thy brother, and

---

37 Translator's note: See Nikodemos the Hagiorite, *Exomologetarion*, 202–230; *Exomologetarion: A Manual of Confession*, 308–343. And Archimandrite Nikodemos Skrettas writes:

> When the term "satisfaction" is used by Nikodemos the Hagiorite in his references pertaining to penances, as is made plainly obvious from the surrounding text it has absolutely no relation to the heretical teaching of Western origin that satisfaction is required on account of man's sins "insulting" divine justice. For St. Nikodemos, "satisfaction" means the penitent's voluntary acceptance and fulfillment of the spiritual penance assigned to him by his Spiritual Father, that is to say, the ascetical rule [*kanon*] given to him after his confession. This spiritual rule is not a juridical penalty or punishment, in order that someone might be satisfied (God, for example, in the present instance, that is, according to the heretical Western theological position). Rather, it is the pedagogical and therapeutic spiritual and bodily exertion by which man is to consciously fulfill his repentance, in theory and in practice. It is the negation of the pleasure of sin, by the grace of God, and the voluntarily accepted therapeutic pain of the repenting person. (*He Theia Eucharistia kai ta Pronomia tes Kyriakes kata te Didaskalia ton Kollybadon* [*The Divine Eucharist and the Prerogatives of Sunday According to the Teaching of the Kollyvades*] [Thessaloniki: Pournaras, 2004], 356)

then come and offer thy gift" (Mt. 5:23–24).[38] Thirdly and finally, this prayer is fitting for those who will commune because of the place where it is recited within the Divine Liturgy, namely, after the catechumens are dismissed and only the faithful remain, after the transubstantiation of the precious Gifts,[39] and before the Church

---

38 Translator's note: And we read in "The Service of Preparation for Holy Communion:"

When thou, O man, art about to eat the Master's Body,

Draw nigh with fear, lest thou be seared; It is Fire.

And as thou drinkest the divine Blood unto communion,

First reconcile thyself with them that grieve thee,

Then, with daring, venture to eat the Mystic Food.

(Symeon Metaphrastes, *Iambici Trimetri*, PG 114, 225B; trans. *A Prayer Book for Orthodox Christians* [Boston: Holy Transfiguration Monastery, 2000], 336–337)

On Great and Holy Thursday St. Proklos of Constantinople preached, "Let us embrace one another from our heart if we intend to approach the divine Mysteries" (*In Sanctum Quintam Feriam* 4, PG 65, 781B). And St. Anastasios of Sinai warned: "Keep far away [from Communion], you who do not forgive your brother" (*Oratio de Sacra Synaxi*, PG 89, 841C).

39 Translator's note: Concerning the use of the Western scholastic term "transubstantiation" by the *Kollyvades* Fathers, Archimandrite Nikodemos Skrettas writes:

The interchangeability in their texts of the terms "transmutation" (or "change") [*metabole*] and "transubstantiation" [*metousiosis*] means that, for the *Kollyvades* these two terms have the same exact and Orthodox meaning regarding the actual change of the bread and of the wine.... The Gifts are changed into the very body and blood of Christ, but the manner of this change, as is the case with the incarnation of God the Word, remains inexplicable. The supranatural wonder, which is beyond explanation, and which is brought about by the working of the Holy Spirit in the Mystery of the Eucharist, can be understood only by faith.... Even if the Western term "transubstantiation" slipped into Orthodox writings at a later date and was used by the *Kollyvades*, it was never understood by them in an Aristotelian or scholastic manner. (*He Theia Eucharistia kai ta Pronomia tes Kyriakes kata te Didaskalia ton Kollybadon*, 60–63)

Cf. John of Damaskos:

And now you ask: How does the bread become the body of Christ, and the wine and the water the blood of Christ? And I say to you: The Holy Spirit visits [*epiphoitao*] them and makes [*poieo*] them so in a manner beyond word and mind.... But if you seek the manner of how it happens, it is sufficient for you to hear that it is by the Holy Spirit. (*Expositio Fidei* 4.86, PG 94, 1141A and 1145A; NPNF [V2-09], 83)

Note that throughout the history of the Orthodox Church, many different terms have been used by many different Fathers and ecclesiastical writers to express (though not define or explain) the actual and real change that takes place in the Mystery: **an anointing** (*chrisis*

calls forth those faithful prepared to commune by crying out: "With the fear of God, with faith, and with love, draw near." That is to say: "Be ready and approach, brethren, in order to receive the superessential bread, the body and blood of His Son, which the heavenly Father desires to give to you today."

We have divided, therefore, the present book into three parts. In the first part we will be concerned with this preparatory prayer of the Lord. In the second part we will occupy ourselves with the subject of frequent Communion. And in the third part we will respond to the objections raised by those who oppose it.

– Theodore of Mopsuestia, Catechetical Homily 16.12, ST 145, 553); **a becoming** (*genesis* – Serapion of Thmuis, "Prayer of the Offering," *The Sacramentary of Serapion* [Thessaloniki: 1967], 125), **a blessing** (*eulogia* – Divine Liturgy of St. Basil the Great: "And bless [these Gifts] and sanctify them and show them to be…"), **a bringing into sight** (*hyp' opsin agoge* – Dionysios the Areopagite, *De Ecclesiastica Hierarchia* 3.3.12–13, PG 3, 444A–444C); **a completion** (*teleiosis* – Germanos of Constantinople, *Historia Ecclesiastica, et Mystica Contemplatio* PG 98, 437A); **a consecration** (*hierourgia* – Gregory of Nyssa, *In Baptismum Christi*, PG 46, 581C); **a conversion** (*conversio* – Ambrose of Milan, *De Sacramentis* 4.5.23, SC 25bis, 114); **a divinization** (*theourgia* – Theodore the Studite, *Epistolarum* 2.203, PG 99, 1617C); **a descending upon/dwelling in** (*epidemia* – Serapion of Thmuis, "Prayer of the Offering," *The Sacramentary of Serapion*, 125); **an immixture** (*emmixis* – Eutychios of Constantinople, *Sermo de Paschate et de Eucharistia* 2, PG 86², 2393C); **a making** (*poiesis* – Cyril of Jerusalem, *Mystagogiae* 5.7, SC 126, 154); **a making-divine** (*theopoiesis* – Symeon the New Theologian, *Ethical Discourses* 3, SC 122, 428); **a manifestation** (*apophansis* – Irenaios of Lyons, *Fragmenta* 38, PG 7, 1253B); **a mutation** (*mutatio* – Ambrose of Milan, *De Mysteriis* 9.52, SC 25bis, 186); **a sanctification** (*hagiasmos* – Mark of Ephesos, *De Corpore et Sanguine Christi*, PG 160, 1080A); **a sending upon** (*katapempsis* – Divine Liturgy of St. John Chrysostom); **a showing forth** (*anadeixis* – Basil the Great, *De Spiritu Sancto* 27.66, SC 17bis, 480); **a transelementation** (*metastoicheiosis* – Gregory of Nyssa, *Oratio Catechetica* 37, PG 45, 97B); **a transformation** (*metaskeue* – John of Damaskos, *Vita Barlaam et Joasaph*, PG 96, 1032A); **a transmutation** (*metabole* – Divine Liturgy of St. John Chrysostom; Theodoret of Cyr, *Eranistes* 1, PG 83, 56B); **a transorientation** (*metarrythmisis* – John Chrysostom, *De Proditione Iudae* 1.6, PG 49, 380); **a transubstantiation** (*metousiosis* – Gennadios Scholarios, *De Sacramentali Corpore Christi* 1, PG 160, 360C); **a transversion** (*metapoiesis* – Cyril of Alexandria, *In Mattheum* 26.27, PG 72, 452C); **a uniting** (*syzeuxis* – Samonas of Gaza, *De Sacramento Altaris*, PG 120, 829B); **a visitation** (*epiphoitesis* – John Chrysostom, *On John* 45.2, PG 59, 253).

The Communion of the Apostles

I am the living bread which came down from heaven: if any man eat of this bread, he shall live for ever: and the bread that I will give is my flesh, which I will give for the life of the world.
Jn. 6:51

Work of Philotheos Skoufos, 1665. Monastery of the Most Holy Theotokos Kassopitras, Corfu.

PART ONE

EXPLANATION OF THE LORD'S PRAYER

FOREWORD TO THE LORD'S PRAYER

The Lord's Prayer, my brothers, according to St. Maximos, includes seven lofty subjects: theology, sonship, equality with the angels, the enjoyment of eternal life, the restoration of human nature, the destruction of the law of sin, and the abolition of the tyranny of the devil.[40] The beginning of the "Our Father" includes the subjects of theology and sonship, for it simultaneously teaches us that God is by nature the Father of the Son and the Emitter [*Proboleus*] of the Holy Spirit,[41] and that, according to creation and grace, He is our Father, and we His sons. The words, "Thy will be done, on earth as it is in heaven," include the subject of equality with the angels, by which words we ask to be united with the angels, and, just as the will of God in heaven is done by the angels in heaven, so also must His will be done by us who are on the earth. The phrase, "Give us this day our superessential bread," includes the subject of the enjoyment of eternal life. The restoration and union of human nature is attested to by the words, "And forgive us our

---

40 Cf. *Orationis Dominicae Expositio*, PG 90, 876B–876C = *GrPhilokalia*, 441; *The Philokalia*, vol. 2 (1981), 287.

41 Translator's note: In his *Third Theological Oration*, St. Gregory the Theologian writes: This is what we mean by Father and Son and Holy Spirit: the Father is the Begetter [*Gennetor*] and the Emitter [*Proboleus*], without passion of course, and without reference to time, and not in a corporeal manner. The Son is the Begotten [*Gennema*], and the Holy Spirit the Emission [*Problema*]; for I know not how this could be expressed in terms altogether excluding visible things. (*Oratio* 29.2, PG 36, 76B; trans. NPNF [V2-07], 301)

debts, as we forgive our debtors," for, when we forgive our enemies, we are united and no longer divided because of a difference of opinion and will. The distancing of sin far from us is disclosed by the words, "And lead us not into temptation," and by saying this we ask that we not enter into temptation proceeding from the law of sin. And the phrase, "But deliver us from the evil one," represents the destruction of the devil's tyranny.

. This teaching of our Lord is called a prayer because it encompasses all that man should ask from God, and all that is fitting for God to give to man. The prayer is divided into three parts: 1) doxology and praise of God; 2) thanksgiving to God for His past, present, and future blessings; and 3) supplication for the forgiveness of our sins and for the sins of our brethren, and various other supplications. The Lord's Prayer contains seven subjects, as we previously said, and is therefore also divided into seven parts. But why seven? This is because man has permission to ask and receive from God during this present, seventh, age; while in the eighth age, that is, the future age, we will not be able to do this, for then it will no longer be time for work, but for the recompense for our actions.

CHAPTER 1

Our Father Who art in the heavens

In truth, my brothers, great is the compassion of our Lord. Inexpressible is the philanthropy which He has shown and does show towards us, who are ungrateful and thankless for His beneficence. For not only did He, out of His infinite goodness, raise us up who had fallen into sin, but He also delivered laws of prayer to us which both direct us towards God and benefit the human race, so that we might not fall again into the same sins on account of foolishness. For this reason, as is proper, the very beginning of the Lord's Prayer elevates our intellect to the highest principle of theology, pointing us towards His Father, the Creator of all the visible and invisible creation, and indicating the sonship of which Christians were deemed worthy, calling Him "Father" by grace.

For since our Lord Jesus Christ became incarnate, He gave the power to all, as many as believed in Him, to become children and sons of God through Holy Baptism, as John the Theologian says: "To them gave He power to become the sons of God, even to them that believe on His Name" (Jn. 1:12). And the Apostle Paul writes: "For ye are all the children of God by faith in Christ Jesus" (Gal. 3:26). And again: "And because ye are sons, God hath sent forth the Spirit of His Son into your hearts, crying, Abba, Father" (Gal. 4:6). That is to say, all faithful Orthodox Christians are children of God through faith and by the grace of Jesus Christ. And again, since you are children of God, He, Who is your Father by grace, sent into your hearts the Holy Spirit of His Son, Who mystically cries out from there: "O Father, our Father."

For this reason our Lord tells us how we should pray towards our Father by grace, so that we may always be kept under the grace of sonship, until the very end, that is, that we may be children of God, not only according to our baptismal rebirth, but also according to our works and actions. For anyone who does not perform spiritual works worthy of the rebirth from above, but rather satanic works, such a person is not worthy to call God his Father, but he is to call the devil his father, according to the saying of our Lord: "Ye are of your father the devil, and the lusts of your father ye will do" (Jn. 8:44). That is to say, you are born according to the evil of your father the devil, and you love to do his evil lusts.

The Lord directs us to call God "Father," on the one hand in order to assure us that we have truly been born as children of God by the rebirth of divine Baptism, and on the other hand because we must also preserve the characteristics, that is, the virtues of our Father. We will accomplish this by feeling constraint in a way because of the kinship we have with Him, as He Himself says: "Be ye therefore merciful, as your Father also is merciful" (Lk. 6:36). That is, be compassionate towards everyone, just as your Father is compassionate towards everyone. And the Apostle Peter says:

> Wherefore gird up the loins of your mind, be sober, and hope to the end for the grace that is to be brought unto you at the revelation of Jesus Christ; as obedient children, not

fashioning yourselves according to the former lusts in your ignorance. But as He which hath called you is holy, so be ye holy in all manner of conversation; because it is written, Be ye holy; for I am holy.[42] And if ye call on the Father, who without respect of persons judgeth according to every man's work, pass the time of your sojourning here in fear. (1 Pet. 1:13–17)

And Basil the Great says: "The mark of the person born of the Spirit is that he should be, according to the measure granted to him, that very thing of which he was born, as it is written: 'That which is born of the flesh is flesh; and that which is born of the Spirit is spirit' (Jn. 3:6)."[43] That is to say, the mark of the person born of the Holy Spirit is that he becomes, as much as possible, like unto the Spirit from Whom he was born, just as it is written: that the person born from a fleshly father is also fleshly himself, that is, carnal, but the person born from the Holy Spirit is also himself spirit, that is, spiritual.

Third, we call Him "Father," since, because we believed in the Only-begotten Son of God, we were reconciled with God our heavenly Father, having previously been His enemies and children of wrath.[44] So by saying "Our Father," He showed that as many as are reborn through Holy Baptism are genuine brothers and children of one Father, that is, children of God and of one Mother, the Holy Eastern, Apostolic, and Catholic Church. Therefore, we must each of us love one another as genuine brothers, as the Lord commands us: "This is My commandment... that ye love one another" (Jn. 15:12, 17).

According to our being, that is, according to our formation and creation, God is and is called the Father of all men, both of believers and of unbelievers. We, then, are obligated to love all men, since they are honored and fashioned by the hands of God. Only evil

---

42 Lev. 11:44–45.

43 *Moralia* 80.22, PG 31, 869A; *Saint Basil: Ascetical Works*, (Washington, D.C.: The Catholic University of America Press, FC, 1962), 204.

44 Cf. Rom. 5:10, Eph. 2:3.

and impiety should we hate, and not anything fashioned by God. And according to well-being, namely, according to the re-formation of Baptism,[45] we Orthodox Christians must love one another even more, because we are doubly united, according to nature and according to grace.

All men are divided into three groups: genuine servants, illegitimate servants, and evil servants who are enemies of and opposed to God. Genuine servants are those who believe correctly and who do the will of God with fear and joy. Illegitimate servants are those who believe in Christ and have received Holy Baptism, but do not do His commandments. The others, however, who are also servants (being creations of God), are evil, enemies of and opposed to God, even if they are very weak and cannot do anything against Him. These are those people who believed in Christ, but afterwards fell into various heresies. Together with these are numbered others, the unbelievers and the impious. We, however, who were deemed worthy to become servants and sons of God by grace through the rebirth of Holy Baptism, let us not again become servants of our enemy the devil by voluntarily falling to his evil wishes, so that we do not become like those concerning whom the Apostle wrote: "Who are taken captive by him (the devil) at his will" (2 Tim. 2:26), namely, ensnared by the devil to do his will.

But, since our Father is in the heavens, we also must look with our intellect upon heaven, there where our fatherland is, the upper Jerusalem; and must not look upon the earth like swine, but upon our sweetest Savior and Master and upon the heavenly beauties of Paradise. And we must not only do this during the time of prayer, but at every moment and in every place we must have our intellect in heaven, so that it may not be scattered among the corruptible and

---

45 Translator's note: The Fathers of the Church speak of "being," "well-being," and "eternal well-being". Man's biological birth and existence is called "being," his baptismal rebirth by grace is called "well-being," and his birth into eternal life in the general resurrection (should he be so fortunate) is called "eternal well-being." Cf. Maximos the Confessor, *Ambiguorum Liber*, PG 91, 1325B-1325C, and Gregory the Theologian, *Oratio* 40.2, PG 36, 360C-361A (NPNF [V2-07], 360).

temporal things here below.[46] And if we force ourselves daily as the Lord says—"The kingdom of heaven suffereth violence, and the violent take it by force" (Mt. 11:12)—that is, the kingdom of heaven is the return for ascetical force, and as many as force themselves, will gain it with the help of God—we will keep the image of God in us whole and pure. Then, slowly but surely, we will raise the image as much as possible to the likeness, being hallowed by God; and we in turn will hallow His divine Name upon the earth, saying the words of the prayer,

CHAPTER 2

Hallowed be Thy Name

Perhaps the Name of God is not holy, and for this reason we must ask for it to be hallowed? How can this be? Is He not the fount of holiness? Is not everything made holy by Him, both heavenly and earthly things? So how is it that the Lord now tells us to hallow His Name? The Name of God, in and of itself, is holy and above-holy and the fount of holiness, and as soon as it is named, everything for which it is called upon is hallowed, while it itself does not sustain any increase or decrease in holiness. However, God desires and wishes that His Name be glorified by all of His creatures, just as the Prophet and Psalmist David says: "Bless the Lord, all ye His works" (Ps. 102:20). And He demands this not so much for His sake, but so that they may be hallowed by Him and glorified. For this reason, no matter what we do, all must be done for the glory of God, according to the Apostle: "Whatsoever ye do, do all to the glory of God" (1 Cor. 10:31). That is, whether you are eating, or drinking, or anything else, do all things for the glory of God, so that the Name of God may be hallowed also by us.

And it is hallowed when we do good and holy works, just as our faith is holy. When men see our good way of life, faithful Christians give glory to God Who grants us wisdom and strengthens us to do good, while unbelievers come to the knowledge of the truth, seeing

---

46 Cf. Col. 3:2.

how our works confirm our faith, just as the Lord commands us, saying: "Let your light so shine before men, that they may see your good works, and glorify your Father which is in heaven" (Mt. 5:16).

If we do the opposite, the Gentiles blaspheme the Name of God because of us, according to the Apostle: "The name of God is blasphemed among the Gentiles through you, as it is written" (Rom. 2:24; Is. 52:5), and this will receive great punishment and is a fearful danger, since men, and especially the unbelievers, believe that whatever we do is what God has commanded us. Therefore, in order not to bring insult and dishonor to God and eternal punishment to ourselves, we must be diligent to couple with correct faith and piety a virtuous life and manner of living. A virtuous life is for us to fulfill the commandments of Christ, just as He says: "If ye love Me, keep My commandments" (Jn. 14:15). And this is so that, by keeping His commandments, we may show the love we have for Him, and so that our faith may be made firm. For the divine Chrysostom says:

> If someone cannot even say "Lord Jesus" except by the Holy Spirit, much more then will he be unable to keep his faith secure and rooted without the Holy Spirit. How, then, can we receive the help of the Spirit and compel Him to remain with us? Through good works and an excellent life. For just as the light of a lantern is fueled by oil, and when the oil burns off the light is extinguished as well; in like manner, the grace of the Spirit ignites and illumines us when we have good works and have much almsgiving and compassion for the poor in our soul. When these are absent, however, then does grace also disappear and depart…. Let us possess the fire of the Spirit through bountiful philanthropy and generous almsgiving, in order that we may not be shipwrecked in regards to faith, for faith requires the help of the Spirit to remain steadfast. And the support given to us by the Spirit is retained and remains on account of a pure life and a virtuous manner of living. If, then, we wish for faith to be rooted within us, we need to live a pure life. This convinces the Spirit to remain with us and to preserve

the strength of faith, for it is impossible for someone who lives an impure life not to waver in the faith.... And for you to learn that this is true, and that evil deeds undermine the firmness of faith, listen to what Paul writes to Timothy: "That thou mightest war a good warfare, holding faith, and a good conscience (which arises from a correct life and good works), which some, having put away their conscience, have made shipwreck of their faith" (1 Tim. 1:18–19). And again he says elsewhere: 'The love of money is the root of all evil, which while some coveted after, they have erred from the faith' (1 Tim. 6:10). Do you see that both those who did not have a good conscience and those who loved avarice placed their faith in danger? We should think upon all these things carefully, taking care to live an excellent life, so that our reward may be double, the one for our good works, and the other for our steadfastness in the faith. For what food is to the body, a virtuous life is to the soul. Just as the nature of our body is such that it cannot live without food, so likewise faith cannot survive without good works, for "faith without works is dead." (Jas. 2:26)[47]

Do you see that both those who do not have a good conscience and those who love money place their faith in danger? Therefore, my brothers, think about all of these things well, and let us diligently strive to lead a virtuous life in order that our reward may be double: one for our good works, and the other for the steadfastness of our faith. For, just as food is necessary for the body, in like manner is a virtuous life necessary for faith. And just as the nature of our body cannot survive without sustenance, so also is faith dead without works. For many received faith and were Christians, but, because they did not have good works to follow their faith, they lost salvation. Let us, however, attend to both faith and good works, so that we may be able without fear to say the rest of the Lord's Prayer,

---

47 *De Verbis Apostoli, Habentes Eumdem Spiritum* 1.5–6, 9–10, PG 51, 276–277, 280–281.

CHAPTER 3

Thy kingdom come

Because human nature by its own will became enslaved to the man-slaying devil, our Lord commands us to ask our God and Father to liberate us from the bitter tyranny of the devil. This will not happen in any other way except if the kingdom of God, which is the Holy Spirit, should come to us, in order to drive away from us the tyrannical enemy and for the Spirit to rule us. And it is proper for the perfect to ask for the kingdom of God the Father, because they have arrived at the perfection of spiritual maturity.[48] But as many of us that still have a convicting conscience, as I do, are not even able to open our mouths and ask for such things, but we must ask God to send the Holy Spirit in order to enlighten us and to strengthen us in His holy will and in works of repentance, for the honorable Forerunner says: "Repent ye; for the kingdom of heaven is at hand" (Mt. 3:2). It is as if he is saying to us: "O men, repent of the evil which you do, and prepare yourselves to receive the kingdom of the heavens, namely, the Only-begotten Son and Word of God, Who came to rule and save the entire world." For this reason, according to the divine Maximos, we must say: "May Thy Holy Spirit come"[49] and purify us completely, both body and soul, so that we may receive and become a worthy dwelling place of the whole Holy Trinity, in order for God to reign in us henceforth, that is, in our hearts, as it is written: "The kingdom of God is within you" (Lk. 17:21). And in another place the Lord says: "I and My Father will come unto him, and make Our abode with him" (Jn. 14:23); namely, I and My Father will come and dwell in him who loves My commandments. Sin must no longer live and reign in us, as the Apostle says: "Let not sin therefore reign in your mortal

---

48 Cf. Eph. 4:13.

49 *Orationis Dominicae Expositio*, PG 90, 884A = *GrPhilokalia*, 443; *The Philokalia*, vol. 2, 290–291. Cf. Gregory of Nyssa, *De Oratione Dominica* 3, PG 44, 1157C and 1160D. [Translator's note: Some ancient manuscripts actually do read, "May Thy Holy Spirit come upon us and purify us," for Lk. 11:2. See *Greek–English New Testament* (Stuttgart: Nestle-Aland, 1998), 195.]

body, that ye should obey it in the lusts thereof" (Rom. 6:12). And being thus strengthened by the presence of the Holy Spirit, we carry out the will of our heavenly God and Father, and, without shame, we say,

CHAPTER 4

Thy will be done, on earth as it is in heaven

There is no more blessed or peaceful thing either in heaven or on earth than for someone to do the will of God. Lucifer was in heaven, but, not wishing to do the will of God, he was cast down to Hades. Adam was in Paradise, honored like a king by all of creation, but because he did not keep the divine commandment he fell into the uttermost privation. Therefore, everyone who does not wish to do the will of God is entirely prideful. For this reason, the Prophet David justly curses them, saying: "Thou hast rebuked the proud; cursed are they that decline from Thy commandments," and, "The proud have transgressed exceedingly" (Ps. 118:21, 51).

By this the Prophet shows that the cause of lawlessness is pride, and the cause of pride is lawlessness. For this reason it is impossible to find a humble man among lawless men, or a man who keeps the law among the proud, for pride is the beginning and the end of all evil. The will of God is that we desist from evil and do good, as the same Prophet says: "Turn away from evil, and do good" (Ps. 33:14). "Good" are those things attested to as such by Holy Scripture and the Saints of the Church, and not whatever each person might foolishly claim, for many times what people say is "good" is in fact harmful and steers man towards perdition.

If we walk according to the world and according to our own lust, we Christians will not in any way differ from the unbelieving Gentiles, who do not have a law and the Scriptures. Neither will we differ from those people who lived during the time of anarchy, as it is written in the book of Judges: "Every man did that which was right in his own eyes, for there was no king in those days" (Jg. 17:6).

For this reason, when the Jews wanted to put our Lord to death on account of their envy,[50] and Pilate wanted to release Him—for he found no crime in Him worthy of death—they responded and said: "We have a law, and by our law He ought to die, because He made Himself the Son of God" (Jn. 19:7). But they were lying when they said this. For where is it found in the Law that whoever calls himself a son of God must be put to death? Rather, the divine Scripture indeed calls men gods and sons of God: "I said: Ye are gods, and all of you the sons of the Most High" (Ps. 81:6). Such a law, then, does not exist.

Do you see, beloved, that they made their envy and their wickedness into a law? Concerning such we read in the Wisdom of Solomon, "But let our law be our might," and, "Let us lie in wait for the righteous man" (Wis. 2:11, 12). The Law and the Prophets certainly write that the Christ will come to take on flesh and die for the life and salvation of the world, but not according to the purposes of those lawless men.

Therefore, so that we may not suffer the same fate, let us heed the commandments of our Lord and not walk outside of that which is written. And His commandments are not burdensome, as the Evangelist John says.[51] But since our Lord always did the will of the Father upon the earth, we must also ask Him to give us strength and enlighten us so that we can do His holy will upon the earth as well, just as the holy angels do it in heaven, for without Him we can do nothing.[52] Just as the angels submit to all of the divine commands without disputation, so should all of us men in like manner submit to the divine will, which is contained within the Scriptures, so that there may be peace upon the earth among men just as there is in heaven among the angels, and so that we may be able to say to Him with boldness,

---

50 Cf. Mt. 27:18, Mk. 15:10.

51 Cf. 1 Jn. 5:3.

52 Cf. Jn. 15:5.

CHAPTER 5

Give us this day our superessential bread

The bread is called superessential in three ways. So that we may understand what bread we are asking for from God when we pray, let us examine each. First, common bread, which is food for the body, is called superessential [daily or necessary] bread. This common bread is mixed with the essence of the body in order to fortify and augment foods which are for the nourishment and well-being of the body. Concerning these things the Apostle James says: "Ye ask, and receive not, because ye ask amiss, that ye may consume it upon your lusts" (Jas. 4:3). And again he says: "Ye have lived in pleasure on the earth, and been wanton; ye have nourished your hearts, as in a day of slaughter" (Jas. 5:3). In other words, "You have lived upon the earth in luxury and comfort. You have fed your bodies so much that it is as though you were preparing them for slaughter."

Our Lord also says to us: "And take heed to yourselves, lest at any time your hearts be overcharged with surfeiting, and drunkenness, and cares of this life, and so that day come upon you unawares" (Lk. 21:34). Which is to say, "Attend to yourselves carefully so that your intellect does not become weighed down with drunkenness and worldly concerns, and so that last day does not come upon you suddenly."

For this reason, we must ask only for that food which is necessary. For the Lord, condescending to our weakness, instructs that we ask for bread, but only for the superessential bread, and not for what is superfluous. Thus, He did not need to say, "Give us *this day*," in addition to the phrase "our superessential bread." Rather, the phrase "this day," according to the interpretation of the divine Chrysostom,[53] means "always." (Thereby, this verse has a succinct character.)

The divine Maximos says that the body is a friend of the soul.[54] Solomon admonishes the soul not to tend to its body with two feet,

---

53 Cf. *On Matthew* 55.5, PG, 58, 547; NPNF [V1-10], 329.

54 Cf. *Orationis Dominicae Expositio*, PG 90, 900C = *GrPhilokalia*, 450; *The Philokalia*, vol. 2, 300.

that is, not to be overly concerned with it, but rather to tend to its body with only one foot, and infrequently at that. This, he says, is so that the body may not become satiated and rise up against the soul, and then do the same evil things which our enemies the demons do against us.[55]

Let us also heed the Apostle, who says: "And having food and raiment let us be therewith content. But they that will be rich fall into temptation and a snare, and into many foolish and hurtful lusts, which drown men in destruction and perdition" (1 Tim. 6:8–9).[56]

But someone might say that, since the Lord directs us to ask for necessary food from God, we should sit without care and be idle, waiting for God to give us food to eat. To such a person we reply that concern and worry are one thing, while work is another. Concern is distraction and disturbance of the intellect "about many things" (Lk. 10:41). Work is for someone to labor, that is, to sow or be occupied with some other craft. However, his intellect is not to be concerned and worried, but he is to have all of his hope in God and to be concerned only with Him, according to the Prophet David, who says: "Cast thy care upon the Lord, and He will nourish thee" (Ps. 54:25). But if someone places his hope in his handicraft, in his labors, or in men, he will hear what the Prophet Moses says in the Law: "Whatsoever goes upon its paws is unclean; and whatsoever has many feet is unclean; and whatsoever goes on all fours continuously is unclean" (cf. Lev. 11:27, 42). This means that whoever hopes in his hands is unclean, and whoever has many concerns is unclean, and whoever continuously goes on all fours is also unclean. According to St. Neilos, he who places all his hope in his own hands, that is, in his handiwork and craft, goes on his hands. He who hopes in sensible things and has his intellect devoted to concern for them walks on all fours. And he who has all of his members bound by bodily things, and with both hands and all of his strength holds them tight, is he who has many feet: "Now the

---

55 Cf. Pr. 7:11; 25:16–17; Neilos the Ascetic, *Liber de Monastica Exercitatione* 14, PG 79, 736D–737A = *GrPhilokalia*, 173; *The Philokalia*, vol. 1 (1979), 209.

56 This, however, does not mean that one must have the same garment and covering his entire life. Rather, when it becomes worn out through use, let him make another one.

phrase 'goes upon his paws' indicates someone who relies on his own hands and places all his hope in them, while to 'go on all fours' is to trust in sensory things and continually to seduce one's intellect into worrying about them; and to have 'many feet' signifies clinging to material objects."[57] The Prophet Jeremiah curses such a person saying: "Cursed is the man that trusteth in man, and will lean his arm of flesh upon him, while his heart departeth from the Lord. But blessed is the man that trusteth in the Lord, and whose hope the Lord is" (Jer. 17:5, 7).

Men! Why are we troubled in vain? The span of our life is so short, as the Prophet David says to God:

> Behold, Thou hast made my days as the spans of a hand, and my being is as nothing before Thee. Nay, all things are vanity, every man living. Surely man walketh about like a phantom, nay, in vain doth he disquiet himself. He layeth up treasure, and knoweth not for whom he shall gather it. (Ps. 38:6–9)

In other words, "Behold, Lord, You have made my days so short, like the length of one hand. And the substance of my nature is nothing compared to Your eternity. Not only I, but everything, is vanity, and every man who lives in the world." Indeed, pitiful man finds himself in this life, not truly, but like a painted image. Yet, even for all this, he unsettles himself from top to bottom in vain, storing away gold and silver; and he, wretched man, does not know for whom he gathers. Come to your senses, O man, and stop running about all day like a madman because of your many concerns, and sitting at night and counting your demonic interest and profits. Indeed, you waste almost your entire life on the riches of mammon, your unjust profits, and you do not even find one free hour to consider your sins and weep over them. Do you not hear our Lord, Who says that "no man can serve two lords" and that "ye cannot serve God and mammon" (Mt. 6:24)? That is, no one can serve two masters, namely, God and unjust riches. And concerning the seed

---

57 *Liber de Monastica Exercitatione* 14, PG 79, 736C–737A = *GrPhilokalia,* 172–173; *The Philokalia,* vol. 1, 208–209.

which fell among the thorns, do you not hear when Scripture says that it was choked and did not bear a single fruit—that is to say, that the word of God fell among the worries and concerns for money, and did not bear a single fruit of salvation?[58] Do you not see this man and that man, once rich, who did the same things that you do, and accumulated a great amount of money? But afterwards God blew it out of their hands and they lost it, and together with it lost their minds, and now they walk about madly, as if possessed by demons. And this happened to them justly, for they had money as their god, and their intellects were devoted to it. Thus, when their god left them, it took with it their minds.

Listen, O man, to what our Lord says to us: "Lay not up for yourselves treasures upon the earth, where moth and rust doth corrupt, and where thieves break through and steal" (Mt. 6:19). And you must do as He says, so that you do not hear from the Lord those terrible words which He said to the rich man: "Thou fool, this night thy soul shall be required of thee; then whose shall those things be, which thou hast provided?" (Lk. 12:20).

Let us come before our God and Father and cast before Him all of our cares of this life, and He will take care of us, as the chief Apostle Peter says.[59] And let us draw near to Him, as the Prophet cries to us: "Come unto Him, and be enlightened, and your faces shall not be ashamed" (Ps. 33:5); that is, approach God and you will be enlightened, and your faces will not be ashamed during a time of need, because you were not helped.

Behold, with the help of God, we have spoken about one explanation of the superessential bread.

Second, the superessential bread is the word of God, the truth, as the divine Scripture says: "Man shall not live by bread alone, but by every word that proceedeth out of the mouth of God" (Dt. 8:3; Mt. 4:4; Lk. 4:4).

The word of God is all of the teaching of the Holy Spirit, namely, all of the divine Scripture, both the Old and the New. As

---

58 [43] Cf. Mt. 13:3–7, 22.

59 [44] Cf. 1 Pet. 5:7.

if from a spring, from this Scripture drew all of the Holy Fathers
and teachers of our Church, who water us with the most-pure
streams of their divinely inspired teaching. And we must receive
their teachings and writings as superessential bread, so that our soul
does not die of hunger for the word of life before our body dies, as
happened to Adam on account of his transgressing the divine commandment.

Some people not only do not want to hear the word of God, but
also obstruct others, either by their words or by their bad example,
from hearing it. And some people not only do not contribute to
the building of schools and other projects which serve towards the
progress of Christian children, but also obstruct those who would
assist in such things. Furthermore, some priests are negligent
and lazy and do not teach their parishioners the necessary things
for their salvation. And some hierarchs do not teach their flock
the commandments of God and the other necessary things for
salvation, and by their evil life become a scandal and the cause of
the perdition of the simplest Christians. All of these will receive the
"woe!" and the "alas!" of the Pharisees and Scribes, for they shut up
the kingdom of the heavens against men, and neither do they enter
in, nor do they allow them who seek it to enter.[60] For this reason, as
evil stewards, they will be deprived of protecting the people.

Also, teachers who instruct Christian children should emphasize
Christian morals. For what profit is it if someone learns grammar
and the other philosophical subjects, but afterwards is corrupt?
What will his learning do for him then? Or what success can such
a person have, either in spiritual matters or in political affairs?
Certainly none.

Therefore, may God not say to us those same words which He
said to the Jews through the mouth of the Prophet Amos: "Behold,
the days come, saith the Lord God, that I will send a famine in the
land, not a famine of bread, nor a thirst for water, but of hearing the
word of the Lord" (Am. 8:11). This happened to them on account
of their unrepentant will. In order for Him not to say these words
also to us, I say, and in order for such a disastrous calamity not to

---

60 [45] Cf. Mt. 23:13–14; Lk. 11:42–44, 46–47.

come upon us, let each one of us be fed by the word and teaching of God as much as possible, in order that our soul not suffer the most bitter and eternal death. The second meaning of "superessential bread," then, is the word of God, which is so much more necessary than the first kind of bread, inasmuch as the life of the soul is much more necessary than the life of the body.

Third, the superessential bread is the body and blood of the Lord, which differs as much from the word of God as does the sun from a ray. In divine Communion, the Sun that is the whole God-man enters into, mixes with, and leavens the whole man, being He Who illumines, enlightens, and sanctifies all of the powers and senses of the soul and body of man, and refashions him from corruption to incorruption.[61]

Thus the words "superessential bread" primarily and for an especial reason refer to the divine Communion of the all-immaculate body and blood of our Lord Jesus Christ, for it preserves and sustains the essence of the soul, and gives it the strength to do the Master's commandments and everything else, as our Lord says: "For My flesh is meat indeed, and My blood is drink indeed" (Jn.

---

61 Translator's note: Note the beautiful words in praise of Holy Communion by Kallistos and Ignatios Xanthopoulos in ch. 91 of *Directions to Hesychasts*:

Concerning Holy Communion and How Many Good Things Frequent Communion Brings Us When We Receive Communion With a Pure Conscience.

The greatest help and assistance for the purification of the soul, the illumination of the intellect, the sanctification of the body, the divine transformation of these unto immortality, as well as the repulsion of the passions and demons and, above all, for the divine union and supranatural communion and unification with God, is frequent communion in the holy, pure, immortal, and life-giving Mysteries—the precious body and blood of our Lord Jesus Christ, our God and Savior—approached with a heart and disposition as pure as is possible for man. (*GrPhilokalia*, 1090; cf. *Writings From the Philokalia On Prayer Of the Heart* [London: Faber and Faber, 1992], 259)

Also note that this and the following chapter of *Directions to Hesychasts* contain many Patristic quotes pertaining to Holy Communion also found in the present book. This is not surprising, seeing that St. Nikodemos compiled and edited the *Philokalia* just prior to his work on *Concerning Frequent Communion*—which attests to the inseparable link between hesychasm and ecclesial/sacramental life.

6:55), which is to say, My flesh is true food, and my blood is true drink.

If someone is in doubt as to how the body of our Lord is called superessential bread, let him listen to what the sacred teachers of our Church say concerning this. First, the divine Gregory, the illuminator of Nyssa, says: "If he ever comes to himself (like the Prodigal Son), if he longs for the food of his father's house, if he returns to the rich Table, upon which is an abundance of the superessential bread which feeds the hirelings of the Lord...."[62] The hirelings are those who labor in the vineyard of God in hope of the promise, that is, as many as work and till the vineyard of the Lord (which is to say, His commandments) in the hopes of receiving as payment the kingdom of the heavens.

St. Isidore Pelousiotes says: "The prayer which the Lord taught does not contain anything earthly, but everything is heavenly and looks to the profit of the soul, even that which appears to be unimportant and sensible. And it is the opinion of many wise men that the Lord said this prayer for the following reason: in order to teach in a special way about the divine word and bread which nourishes the bodiless soul and which, in some way, is mixed and infused into the essence of the soul. For this reason it is also called superessential bread, inasmuch as the word 'essence' is more becoming of the soul than the body."[63]

The divine Cyril of Jerusalem says: "Common bread is not superessential. But this Holy Bread, appointed for the essence of the soul, is superessential. This bread is diffused throughout your system for the benefit of body and soul."[64]

The divine Maximos says:

> For if we live in the way we have prayed, to nourish our souls and to maintain the good state which we have been granted we will receive the superessential and life-giving bread, that is, the Word, Who said: "I am the bread which came down

62 *In Suam Ordinationem*, PG 46, 548C–548D.

63 *Liber* 2, *Epistola* 281, PG 78, 712B–712C.

64 *Mystagogiae* 5.15, SC 126, 162; NPNF [V2-07], 155.

from heaven and gives life to the world" (cf. Jn. 6:41, 33). He becomes everything for us in proportion to the virtue and wisdom with which we have been nourished.[65]

In other words, living according to the words of the Lord's Prayer, let us receive the Son and Word of God as the superessential bread, as vital food for our souls, and as a safeguard for the goods which have been granted to us. Moreover, the Lord said that He is the bread which came down from the heavens and gives life to the world. However, this occurs within each person who receives Him according to the virtue and knowledge which he has.

And John of Damaskos says: "This bread, which is called superessential, is the first-fruits of the future bread. For 'superessential' means either of the future, which is to say, of the future age, or that which we receive for the constitution of our essence (that is, our body). Whether it be the former or the latter meaning, it is obviously to be called the body of the Lord."[66] Furthermore, the sacred Theophylact also says: "And the body of Christ is superessential bread, which we pray to partake of without condemnation."[67]

Because the Fathers say that the body of the Lord is called superessential bread does not mean that they dismiss the common bread which is given for the sustenance of our body, for this also is a gift of God, and no food is scorned or rejected, according to the Apostle, when it is partaken of and eaten with thanksgiving to God:

---

65 *Orationis Dominicae Expositio*, PG 90, 896D–897A = *GrPhilokalia*, 448; *The Philokalia*, vol. 2, 298. [Translator's note: St. Maximos continues:

The one who prays to receive this superessential bread does not receive it altogether as it is in itself, but according to his own capacity to receive it. For the Bread of Life, out of His love for men, gives Himself to all who ask Him, but not in the same manner to everyone. To those who have done great works of righteousness, He gives Himself more fully; to those who have done smaller ones, less. To each, then, He gives Himself in accordance with the capacity of his intellect. (PG 90, 897B–897C = *GrPhilokalia*, 449; *The Philokalia*, vol. 2, 299). See also *Second Century on Theology* 56, PG 90, 149A–1149B = *GrPhilokalia*, 353; *The Philokalia*, vol. 2, 150–151.]

66 *Expositio Fidei* 4.86, PG 94, 1152B.; NPNF [V2-09], 84.

67 *On Matthew* 6, PG 123, 205A.

"Nothing is to be refused, if it be received with thanksgiving" (1 Tim. 4:4).

However, this common bread is called superessential in a secondary, not primary, sense, for it strengthens only the body and not the soul. But the body of our Lord and the word of God are called superessential bread primarily and in every respect, because they strengthen both soul and body. This is apparent from the example of many men. The Prophet Moses fasted forty days and nights without eating any bodily food. The Prophet Elias likewise fasted for forty days. Under the New Grace a great number of Saints, with only the word of God and Holy Communion, have lived without food for many days. For this reason, as many of us as have been deemed worthy to receive spiritual rebirth through divine Baptism have the need to frequently eat, with fervent love and a broken heart,[68] this spiritual food, in order to live a spiritual life and to keep ourselves unharmed by the poison of the noetic serpent, the devil.[69] If Adam had eaten of this food, he would not have died the double death of the soul and of the body.[70]

We must not eat this spiritual bread, however, without preparation, for our God is called a consuming fire that burns.[71] Holy Communion purifies, illumines, and sanctifies those who eat the Master's body and drink the immaculate blood with a pure conscience and true confession. But it scorches and injures severely the souls and bodies of those who commune unworthily and unconfessed, just as in the case of those who, as the sacred Gospel says, entered the wedding feast not having a garment

---

68 Cf. Ps. 50:17.

69 Translator's note: That the eucharistic body and blood of Christ is an "antidote" and the "medicine of immortality," see Ignatios the Godbearer, *Epistle to the Ephesians* 20, SC 10, 76 (ANF [01], 58), and Gregory of Nyssa, *Oratio Catechetica* 37, PG 45, 93A-93B (NPNF [V2-05], 504).

70 Translator's note: This, in fact, is what St. Maximos the Confessor says: "For if [the first man] had satisfied himself with this divine food, he would not have fallen prey to the death brought in by sin" (*Orationis Dominicae Expositio*, PG 90, 897B = *GrPhilokalia*, 449; *The Philokalia*, vol. 2, 299).

71 Cf. Dt. 4:24.

worthy of the wedding—that is, not having works and fruits worthy of repentance.[72]

And those who listen to satanic songs, gossip, chatter, and other like absurdities are not worthy to listen to the word of God. Likewise, those who lead sinful lives cannot receive Communion and enjoy the immortal life which is brought about by divine Communion, because the powers of their souls have been put to death by the sting of sin.[73] As an analogy, let us consider the members of the body. Inasmuch as the members are able to receive life-giving power, they receive life from the soul. If some member rots or withers, however, it can no longer receive life, for life-giving power does not pass into dead members. In the same fashion, the soul lives inasmuch as it receives the life-giving power from God. But when it sins and becomes unreceptive to the life-giving power, that pitiful soul dies a spiritual death. And, after a time, the body also dies, and the wretched man is completely lost in eternal hell.

We have spoken, then, about the third and final meaning of the superessential bread, which is as necessary and beneficial to us as Holy Baptism is necessary and beneficial. For this reason, we must frequently run to the divine Mysteries and partake of the superessential bread that we ask for from our God and Father, with fear and love, while it is still "today." And "today" has three meanings. First, it means every day. Second, it means the whole life of each person. And third, it means the entire present, seventh age. For in the future age there is no today and tomorrow, but that entire age is one eternal day. Our Lord, knowing that there is no repentance in Hades, and also that it is impossible for us men not to falter after Holy Baptism, teaches us to say to our God and Father,

---

72 Cf. Mt. 22:11–13.
73 Cf. 1 Cor. 15:56.

CHAPTER 6

And forgive us our debts, as we forgive our debtors

It was mentioned above that no one should presumptuously and haphazardly partake of the Holy Bread and sacred Communion, without any preparation. For this reason the Lord now tells us through the Prayer that we must be reconciled with God and with our brothers before approaching the divine Mysteries, just as He says in another place: "If thou bring thy gift to the altar, and there rememberest that thy brother hath ought against thee; leave there thy gift before the altar, and go thy way; first be reconciled to thy brother, and then come and offer thy gift" (Mt. 5:23–24).

Our Lord demonstrates three more things by these words. First, He urges the virtuous to be humble, as He also says in another place: "So likewise ye, when ye shall have done all those things which are commanded you, say, We are unprofitable servants: we have done that which was our duty to do" (Lk. 17:10). Second, He counsels those who have sinned after Baptism not to fall into despair. And third, He shows with these words that He wants us to have compassion and mercy towards one another, for man does not resemble and become like God in any greater way than by showing compassion. For this reason, just as we would have God behave towards us, in the same way must we behave towards our brothers. And let no one say: "So and so wronged me greatly, and I cannot forgive him." For if we considered how many times a day, how many times an hour, how many times each moment we commit faults against God, and He forgives us, we would see how incomparably greater our faults are than those of our brothers. And if the absolute righteousness of God were to make a comparison, it would show that our faults are like the ten thousand talents, while those of our brothers are like the one hundred denarii, that is, as nothing compared to our own.[74] So if we forgive our brothers their few and small faults committed against us, not just with our lips (as many do), but with our whole heart, God will certainly also forgive us our great and innumerable

---

74 Cf. Mt. 18:23–35.

faults committed against Him. But if we do not forgive the faults of our brothers, we profit nothing from our other virtues—whatever virtues we might think we have.

What am I saying—that we will not benefit from our virtues? Indeed, if we do not forgive others we will not even receive forgiveness for our sins, as the Lord decrees: "If ye forgive not men their trespasses, neither will your Father forgive your trespasses" (Mt. 6:15). And again, to whomever does not forgive his co-laborer, He says: "O thou wicked servant, I forgave thee all that debt, because thou desiredst me. Shouldest not thou also have had compassion on thy fellowservant, even as I had pity on thee? And his lord was wroth, and delivered him to the tormentors, till he should pay all that was due unto him. So likewise shall My heavenly Father do also unto you, if ye from your hearts forgive not every one his brother their trespasses" (Mt. 18:32–35).

Many say that sins are forgiven through Holy Communion. Others are opposed to this and say that they are not forgiven through Holy Communion, but only through the Mystery of Confession. We, however, say that both are necessary: preparation through confession and the fulfillment of our rule, and the sacred reception of Holy Communion.[75] For neither to the one nor to the other can we ascribe the whole. Rather, let us consider a dirty garment which, after it has been washed, also requires the warmth of the sun to dry out its moisture and dampness. For if it remains wet, it becomes ruined, and no one can wear it. Or just like a wound, after someone cleanses and disinfects it, killing the worms, and cuts away the dead skin, cannot be left alone without ointment; in the same way, after sin has been washed and cleansed away through

---

75 Translator's note: This is attested to by St. Nicholas Cabasilas:

The sorrow and tears of those who repent of sins after the baptismal washing and entreat for grace stand in need of the blood of the New Covenant and of the body which was slain, since they are of no avail without them…. There is also among the Holy Mysteries that which, when men repent of their sins and confess them to the priests, delivers them from every penalty of God the Judge. Yet even of this Mystery [of Confession] they are not able to obtain the effect unless they feast at the sacred banquet. (*De Vita in Christo* 4, PG 150, 592B; trans. *The Life in Christ* [Crestwood: St. Vladimir's Seminary Press, 1974], 121)

confession, and its deadness cut away through one's ascetical rule, divine Communion is also necessary, to kill it completely and to heal it like an ointment. For without Communion, man reverts to his previous condition, and "the last state of that man becomes worse than the first" (Mt. 12:45), as the Lord says.

For this reason, we must purify ourselves beforehand from all stain through confession, and certainly from rancor and ill feelings towards our brothers, and then draw near to the Holy Mysteries. For just as love is the fulfillment and perfection of the whole Law, the remembrance of wrongs and hatred are the refutation and violation of the whole Law and of every virtue. Wishing to show the evil of the rancorous, the wise Solomon says: "The ways of those that remember wrongs lead to death" (Pr. 12:28), and again: "He that remembers wrongs is a transgressor" (Pr. 21:24).

The wretched Judas had the bitter leaven of rancor in him, and for this reason, after he received the bread, "Satan entered into him" (Jn. 13:27).[76] Let us then be fearful, brothers, of the condemnation and punishment brought about by the remembrance of wrongs, and let us forgive our brothers for whatever faults they have committed against us. And this, not only when we desire to commune, but always, just as the Apostle orders us: "Let not the sun go down upon your wrath" (Eph. 4:26). And again he says: "Neither give place to the devil" (Eph. 4:27). Namely, do not allow the devil to approach, in order that we may be able to say to God with boldness the rest of the Prayer.

CHAPTER 7

And lead us not into temptation

Our Lord directs us to ask our God and Father not to lead us into temptation. The Prophet Isaiah, as representing God, says, "I form the light, and create darkness; I make peace, and create evil" (Is. 45:7). And the Prophet Amos says similarly, "Shall there be evil in a city, and the Lord hath not done it?" (Am. 3:6).

---

76 Cf. Anastasios of Sinai, *Oratio de Sacra Synaxi*, PG 89, 832B–832C.

Based on these words, many unlearned and insecure people fall into various thoughts concerning God: that God supposedly throws us into temptations. For this reason, the Apostle James solved the problem for us, saying: "Let no man say when he is tempted, I am tempted of God: for God cannot be tempted with evil, neither tempteth He any man. But every man is tempted, when he is drawn away of his own lust, and enticed" (Jas. 1:13–14). Therefore, each person, from his own will, is tempted.

Temptations come to man in two kinds. One is the pleasurable kind, and therefore occurs with both our own will and the collaboration of the demons.[77] The other is the sorrowful and painful kind, which appears bitter to us, for it occurs without our will. The devil works on his own to bring about this kind.[78]

Both of these kinds of temptations came upon the Hebrews. For because they willfully chose pleasurable temptation, using wealth, glory, and freedom for evil, they fell into idolatry. For this reason God allowed the complete opposite to come upon them, namely, poverty, dishonor, exile, and the rest. With these evils He frightened them, in order that they might turn and repent.

The Prophets call the various forms of the chastisement of God wrongs and evil, as we said above, though in reality they are not evil, and this is because those things which bring pain and hardship to man are customarily called evil by him, since this is how he perceives them. These things happen, not according to the original will of God, but according to the ensuing [that is, secondary] will of God, for the correction and good of man.

---

77 Translator's note: "Temptation," as it is usually understood in English, is initiated by the demons without our willing it and is called an "assault," for which we are not culpable. Here St. Nikodemos uses the word "temptation" according to the broader meaning that it can possess in Greek, to refer also to our voluntary consent to the assault and our sinful act, for which we are culpable.

78 Cf. Maximos the Confessor, *Orationis Dominicae Expositio*, PG 90, 908B = *GrPhilokalia*, 452–453; *The Philokalia*, vol. 2, 304–305); and *Fifth Century on Various Texts of Theology* 89–94, *GrPhilokalia*, 405–406; *The Philokalia*, vol. 2, 282–283). [Translator's note: This usage of the word "temptation" refers to what is often called a "trial" (e.g. "the trials of Job"): a challenging circumstance that tests one's faith, permitted by God in order to aid one's spiritual progress.]

Our Lord, joining the first kind of temptation (that is, the pleasurable kind) with the second kind (that is, the bitter and oppressive kind) calls both of them by one name, "temptation," because the free will of man is tempted and tested by them. However, in order for us to better understand this, we must know that things are divided into three categories: good, evil, and relative. The good are restraint, almsgiving, righteousness, and as many other like things, which can never be evil. The evil are sexual immorality, inhumanity, injustice, and as many other like things, which can never be good. The relative are wealth and poverty, health and sickness, life and death, glory and ignobility, pleasure and pain, freedom and slavery, and other like things, which at times are good and at times are bad, depending upon how they are used by the free will of man.

Men divide the relative into two. Some they call good, because they desire them (for example, wealth, glory, pleasure, and so on). Others they call evil, because they do not desire them (for example, poverty, pain, dishonor, and the rest). Therefore, if we do not wish for the supposedly evil things to come upon us, let us not do the things that are truly evil, as the Prophet counsels us: "Give not thy foot unto moving, and may he not slumber that guardeth thee" (Ps. 120:3). That is to say, O man, do not walk in the ways of evil and sin, and the angel that guards you will certainly not let you suffer any evil.

Isaiah says: "If ye be willing and obedient, ye shall eat the good of the land. But if ye refuse and rebel, ye shall be devoured with the sword" (Is. 1:19–20). That is to say, if you wish to listen to My commandments, you will enjoy the good things of the earth. But if you do not want to listen to Me, you will die by the sword of your enemy. And if we do not listen, He once more says to us, through the same Prophet, "Walk in the light of your fire, and in the sparks that ye have kindled" (Is. 50:11); that is, "enter into the fire and flame of evils and of hell, which flame you ignited by your sins."

The devil first attacks us with pleasurable temptation, for he knows that we fall into it easily. And if he finds our will obedient to his, he draws us away from the grace of God which protects us. On account of his great hatred for us, he then requests permission from God to bring upon us bitter temptation, that is, sorrows and hardships, in order to destroy us completely and cause us to fall into despair on account of our many sufferings. If he does not find our will compliant, that is, if we do not fall to the pleasurable temptation, he still brings the second kind of temptation, hoping that through many sorrows he will be able to force us to carry out his evil intent.

For this reason, the Apostle Peter directs us: "Be sober, be vigilant; because your adversary the devil, as a roaring lion, walketh about, seeking whom he may devour" (1 Pet. 5:8). God sometimes permits him to do this in order to test His servants, as in the case of Job and the other Saints, in accordance with the Lord's word to His disciples: "Simon, Simon, behold, Satan hath desired to have you, that he may sift you as wheat" (Lk. 22:31). That is, "Behold, Peter, Satan asked permission to sift all of you, to shake you up with temptations as wheat is shaken up." Or God allows temptations by means of His withdrawing, as happened to David because of the sin he committed and to the Apostle Peter because of his arrogance. Other times temptations come on account of God's abandonment, as it happened to Judas and the Jews.

The temptations the saints experience by the permission of God come from the envy of the devil, and are permitted in order that they may manifest saintly righteousness and perfection, and thus shine all the more brightly on account of their victory over their opponent. The temptations which happen by God's withdrawal occur in order to obstruct and cut off past, present, or future sins. The temptations which happen by God's abandonment are caused by the sinful life of man and his evil will, and lead one to complete perdition.

Therefore, not only must we flee, as from venom of the evil serpent, the pleasurable and sinful kind of temptation, but, also, we must not by any means accept temptation of this kind that comes to us without our will. Concerning painful bodily temptations and trials, let us not conduct ourselves haphazardly, with pride and audacity. But let us ask God that they might not come to us, if that is His will, and that we may be pleasing to Him without undergoing these trials. And if they do come, we should accept them with complete thanksgiving and joy, as great blessings. This only should we ask: that He might give us the strength to conquer the tempter until the very end. For this is what "lead us not into temptation" means, that God might not let us fall defeated into the throat of the noetic dragon. In the same way, in another place the Lord tells us: "Watch and pray, that ye enter not into temptation," namely, be alert and constantly praying, so as not to fall into temptation; that is, so as not to be conquered by temptation, "for the spirit is willing, but the flesh is weak" (Mt. 26:41).

Let no one, however, upon hearing that he must flee temptation, "make excuse with excuses in sins" (Ps. 140:4), and claim that he is too weak and other like things when temptations come. For if, during a critical time, he is scared of trial and temptation and does not resist it, he will deny the truth. For example: If the time comes when someone is being tortured for the faith or in order that he might deny the truth or forsake righteousness, compassion, or some other commandment of Christ; if, I say, he surrenders on account of fear of bodily trial, and does not bravely resist, let such a person know that he has no part in Christ, and in vain is he called a Christian, if he does not repent with bitter tears. For he did not imitate the true Christians, the martyrs, who suffered for the faith, such as the divine Chrysostom, who suffered because of his righteousness; the righteous Zotikos, who underwent hardships on account of his compassion;[79] and so many others, which time does not permit us to enumerate, who endured many and great sufferings and temptations for the Law and for the commandments of Christ. These commandments of Christ we also must keep, for they liberate us, not only from temptations and sins, but also from the evil one, according to the petition,

---

79 Translator's note: St. Zotikos, commemorated December 31ˢᵗ, was martyred by the pro-Arian Emperor Constantius II in the fourth century for using money from the imperial treasury to care for plague victims who had been exiled from Constantinople, and to ransom other plague victims who had been condemned to drowning.

CHAPTER 8

But deliver us from the evil one

The "evil one" *par excellence*, my brothers, is the devil himself, for he is the cause and originator of all sin and the creator of every temptation. We are taught to ask God to liberate us from the devil's workings and assaults, believing that He will not allow us to be tempted beyond our strength, as the Apostle says: "But with the temptation He will also make a way to escape, that ye may be able to bear it" (1 Cor. 10:13). It is necessary, however, that we not be negligent to cry out to Him in humility,

CHAPTER 9

Conclusion: "For Thine is the kingdom and the power and the glory, unto the ages. Amen."

Our Lord, knowing that human nature, having little faith, always loses heart, consoles us by saying: "Since you have such a mighty and supremely exalted Father and King, do not doubt concerning those things for which you occasionally ask Him. Only, do not be negligent in bothering Him, just as the widow bothered the unjust judge,[80] and say to God: "O Lord, deliver Thou us from our adversary, for Thine is the everlasting kingdom, Thine the invincible might, and Thine the incomprehensible glory. As a mighty King, Thou rulest over our enemies and dost punish them. As the supremely exalted God, Thou dost glorify and magnify those who glorify Thee. And as a philanthropic and affectionate Father, Thou dost befriend and love all those who have been deemed worthy to become Thy sons through Holy Baptism and to love Thee with all their hearts; both now and ever, and unto the ages of ages. Amen."

---

80 Cf. Lk. 18:1–6.

Afterward to the Lord's Prayer

The Lord's Prayer may be divided into nine sections, just as there are nine orders of the heavenly angels, for this prayer lifts man to the work and dignity of the angels. It may also be divided into three sections: the introduction or prologue, the seven petitions, and the conclusion—as God is three Persons, Father, Son, and Holy Spirit; as there are three orders of the righteous, according to the Parable of the Sower, who bear fruit a hundredfold, sixtyfold, and thirtyfold;[81] as there are three types of spiritual vision [*theoria*] according to the Fathers; namely, the spiritual vision of sensible creatures, the spiritual vision of noetic creatures, and the spiritual vision of the Holy Trinity; and as there were three types of trees in Paradise: one to simply live, one to live well, and one to live well and forever. And there are many other spiritual things represented by the number three.

Beloved, behold the wondrous wisdom of our Lord. He knows that three things save man: faith, action [*praxis*], and spiritual vision. First one believes from hearing, then he takes action and performs the commandments, and finally he is deemed worthy to be united with God through spiritual vision; that is, he experiences through the faith attained by spiritual vision those same things in which he first believed through the faith that comes from hearing. Because the Lord knows this, I say, He composed the Lord's Prayer with wondrous wisdom. He began the Prayer with the subject of theology and established it on faith. He then added the petitions, which are related to doing and practicing the commandments. Finally, He sealed the conclusion also with the subject of theology and faith, because He is the Alpha and the Omega, the beginning and the end of the faithful who are being saved.

The Lord included this teaching in prayer, and not in some other virtue. First, because it was appropriate at that moment, since the Apostles had asked Him to teach them how to pray.[82] And, second,

---

81 Cf. Mt. 13:8.
82 Cf. Lk. 11:1.

because every virtue is acquired through prayer. If someone studies the matter carefully, he will also find love, which is the capital of all the virtues and is always accompanied by prayer. Prayer begins and is perfected through love. And love is strengthened and perfected through prayer.

**Christ the High Priest with the
Three Hierarchs and Saint Hippolytos**

Monastery of Strofadon and Saint Dionysios, Zakinthos.

Detail of Christ the High Priest, Katholicon, Holy Monastery of Stavronikita, Mount Athos.

The Bread Come Down from Heaven

As the living Father hath sent me, and I live by the Father: so he that eateth me, even he shall live by me. This is that bread which came down from heaven: not as your fathers did eat manna, and are dead: he that eateth of this bread shall live for ever.

Jn. 6:57-58

PART TWO

CONCERNING FREQUENT COMMUNION

CHAPTER 1

It Is Necessary for the Orthodox to Partake Frequently of the Divine Body and Blood of Our Lord

All Orthodox Christians are commanded to receive Communion frequently. First, by the orders of our Lord and Master Jesus Christ. Second, by the Acts and Canons of the Holy Apostles and the sacred Councils and by the testimonies of the divine Fathers. Third, by the very words, the order, and the celebration of the Divine Liturgy. Fourth, by Holy Communion in and of itself.

1. Our Lord Jesus Christ, before He handed down the Mystery of Communion, said: "And the bread that I will give is My flesh, which I will give for the life of the world" (Jn. 6:51). This means that, for the faithful, divine Communion is a necessary constituent of the spiritual life in Christ. This spiritual life in Christ is not to be extinguished or interrupted—as the Apostle says: "Quench not the Spirit" (1 Th. 5:19)—but must be continuous and uninterrupted, "that they which live should not henceforth live unto themselves, but unto Him which died for them, and rose again" (2 Cor. 5:15), according to the words of the same Apostle. That is, the living faithful are no longer to live a selfish and carnal life, but the life of

Christ, Who died and resurrected for them. Necessarily, then, it is required that divine Communion, the constituent of this spiritual life, also be uninterrupted.

And in another place the Lord says imperatively: "Verily, verily, I say unto you, Except ye eat the flesh of the Son of Man, and drink His blood, ye have no life in you" (Jn. 6:53). These words make apparent that divine Communion is just as necessary for the Christian as Holy Baptism. For He used the same double expression when speaking about Baptism and about Communion. Concerning Baptism, He said: "Verily, verily, I say unto thee, Except a man be born of water and of the Spirit, he cannot enter into the kingdom of God" (Jn. 3:5). Concerning divine Communion, He likewise said: "Verily, verily, I say unto you, Except ye eat the flesh of the Son of Man, and drink His blood, ye have no life in you" (Jn. 6:53). Therefore, just as without Baptism it is impossible for one to live the spiritual life and be saved, it is impossible for one to live without divine Communion. But since these two have this difference, that Baptism is to occur but one time, while divine Communion is to occur frequently and daily, it is right to conclude that there are two requirements respecting divine Communion: one, that it is to be received; and the other, that it is to be received frequently.

When the Lord handed down this Mystery to His disciples, He did not merely make a recommendation, saying: "Whoever wants to eat My body, and whoever wants to drink My blood"—as He did when He said, "Whoever wants to follow Me,"[83] and, "If you want to be perfect."[84] Rather, He commandingly cried out: "Take, eat; this is My body" (Mt. 26:26), and, "Drink of it, all of you, this is My blood" (Mt. 26:27–28). That is, "You must absolutely eat My body, and you must unfailingly drink My blood." Again He says: "This do in remembrance of Me" (Lk. 22:19). That is, "I am delivering this Mystery to you so that you might celebrate it, not one, two, or three times, but every day (as the divine Chrysostom interprets it),[85]

---

83 Cf. Mt. 16:24.
84 Cf. Mt. 19:21.
85 Cf. *On Ephesians* 3.4–5, PG 62, 29; NPNF (V1-13), 64.

unto the remembrance of My sufferings, My death, and My whole incarnate economy."

Behold how these words of the Lord clearly present the two requirements respecting Communion, the one by the fundamental command they contain, and the other by the frequency signified by the words "this do;" and this clearly means that we are strongly commanded not only to commune, but also to commune often. Everyone, therefore, can now see that an Orthodox is not allowed to transgress these things, no matter his order.[86] Rather, he is absolutely obligated and required to keep them, and to receive them as commands and ordinances of the Master.

2. The divine Apostles, following this commanding directive of our Lord, at the beginning of their preaching gathered together as soon as they could with all of the faithful in a hidden place, for fear of the Jews. There they taught the Christians, praying and celebrating the Mystery, and they and all gathered there with them communed, as the sacred Luke bears witness in the Acts of the Apostles. There, he says that the three thousand people who believed in Christ on the day of Pentecost and were baptized were with the Apostles in order to listen to their teaching and to benefit from it, to pray together, and to commune of the immaculate Mysteries in order to be sanctified and to be more firmly established in the faith of Christ: "And they continued steadfastly in the Apostles' doctrine, and in Communion, and in breaking of bread, and in prayers" (Acts 2:42).

And in order for later Christians to keep this mandatory tradition of the Lord, and in order for it not to be forgotten over time, that which the Apostles practiced they also wrote in their eighth and ninth Canons, commanding in exact detail, and with the threat of the penance of excommunication, that no one is to remain uncommuned of the divine Mysteries: "If anyone… does not receive Communion when the offering is made, let him declare the reason; and, if it is legitimate, let him be excused. But if he does not declare it, let him be excommunicated."[87]

---

86 Translator's note: That is, whether he is ordained, a monastic, or a layperson.

87 Canon 8 of the Holy Apostles (*Pedalion* [Athens: Papademetriou, 2003], 11; *The Rudder,*

And in the ninth Canon they say: "Any of the faithful who enter in and listen to the Scriptures, but do not stay for the prayers and Holy Communion, are to be excommunicated, as causing disorder in the Church."[88] Explaining this Canon, Theodore Balsamon says: "The ordinance of the present Canon is very severe, for it excommunicates those who go to Church but do not remain until the end or receive Communion. And other Canons also designate the same thing, so that all will be prepared and worthy to receive Communion."[89]

Following the sacred Apostles, the Council in Antioch first ratifies the above Canons, and then adds:

> Any who enter the Church of God and listen to the sacred Scriptures, but do not participate in prayer with the people, or who turn away from the Communion of the Eucharist, by reason of some disorder, are to be cast out of the Church until they have made confession, and shown fruits of repentance, and made entreaty, and then they will be able to be forgiven.[90]

My brothers, do you now see that all Christians are subject to mandatory excommunication and must receive Communion frequently? And that they are required to do so at every Divine Liturgy, in order that they not be excommunicated by the sacred Apostles and by the Holy Council?

3. If we look carefully at the sacred Divine Liturgy, we will see that, from beginning to end, it has as its goal and reference the Communion of the gathered faithful Christians. For the prayers which the priest reads silently, those which he says aloud, and, simply, all of the sacred words, rituals, and directions of the Divine Liturgy show this.

[Chicago: The Orthodox Christian Educational Society, 1983], 20).

88 *Pedalion*, 11; *The Rudder*, 21.

89 PG 137, 53B.

90 Canon 2 (*Pedalion*, 407; *The Rudder*, 535).

Concerning the silent prayers, in the Second Prayer of the Faithful it is written: "Grant them (the faithful, that is) always to worship Thee with fear and love, and without guilt and condemnation to partake of the Holy Mysteries." In the prayer recited after the completion of the Mysteries[91] it is written: "That to those who shall partake thereof they may be unto vigilance of soul, unto forgiveness of sins." The prayer before Communion says: "And vouchsafe, by Thy mighty hand, to give to us Thine immaculate body and Thy precious blood, and through us, to all Thy people."

Concerning those things which are said aloud, the priest, as if the Lord is speaking, cries out to the people, "Take, eat; this is My body," and, "Drink of it, all of you, this is My blood." Holding the sacred chalice containing the life-giving body and blood, the priest exits from the sanctuary and holds it up for all the people to see. He then calls them to divine Communion, shouting aloud: "With the fear of God, with faith, and with love, draw near." That is, come forth in order to receive, with the fear of God, with faith and love, the divine Mysteries.

After Communion, the priest and the people thank God that they have been deemed worthy of this great grace. The people offer thanksgiving: "Let our mouths be filled with Thy praise, O Lord... for Thou hast deemed us worthy to partake of Thy holy, immortal, and immaculate Mysteries." The priest says: "Upright, having received the divine, holy, immaculate, and life-giving Mysteries, let us worthily give thanks to the Lord." Namely, "O brothers, since we have all received the holy and life-giving Mysteries with an upright conscience, let us with one voice give thanks to the Lord for this."

If one considers the Cherubic Hymn which is chanted by the people, he will see that it too is a preparation for Communion. For it says that all of us, who mystically represent the many-eyed Cherubim, and who chant the thrice-holy hymn to the life-giving Trinity, are to cast out from our intellect every concern and care of this life, because we are going to partake of and receive into our soul the King of all, Who is invisibly surrounded by the orders of the heavenly angels.

---

91 Translator's note: That is, after the sanctification of the Holy Gifts.

The Lord's Prayer, which is recited after the transubstantiation of the Mysteries, also indicates this. For by this prayer Christians ask from God the Father to give them the superessential bread, which is primarily Holy Communion, as we said earlier, in the first part of this book. Even the names by which the Divine Liturgy is especially called, that is, "Communion" and "Synaxis" [that is, "Gathering"], refer in some way to frequent Communion. For "Communion" and "Synaxis" denote that, through the reception of the body and blood of Christ, all the faithful are gathered together in communion and are united with Christ, and they become one body and one spirit with Him.[92]

So, based on all of these sacred rituals of the Divine Liturgy, I ask you, my brothers, to tell me in the fear of God and in the good conscience of your soul, is it not obvious that Christians who attend the Liturgy are required to commune frequently? Are they not obligated to do this in order to show that it is a communion, a gathering, and a supper, and so that they may not be shown to be transgressors of those very things which they believe and confess during the Liturgy? If, however, they do not receive Communion as they have confessed during the Liturgy, I fear, I truly fear, that they might be found to be transgressors. But also, regarding the priest's call to them to come forward, and the other sacred words, acts, and rituals which take place during the Divine Liturgy—I no longer know if they are even in their correct places. For every single person withdraws, so that not even a single Christian is found to approach the Holy Mysteries, to obey such an invitation from the priest—or, to state it better, from God. But rather, the priest, having done nothing, turns back with the Holy Things, without anyone having accepted his invitation to come forward and receive Communion.

---

92 Cf. Eph. 4:4. [Translator's note: That the faithful who partake of the deified body of Christ in the Eucharist are transformed into that very immortal and incorruptible body, thus truly becoming one body with Him, see Justin Martyr, *Apologia* 1.66, PG 6, 428C-429A (ANF [01], 185), Gregory of Nyssa, *Oratio Catechetica* 37, PG 45, 93A-93B (NPNF [V2-05], 504-505), and Cyril of Alexandria, *In Joannis Evangelium* 4.2, PG 73, 577B-580A.]

For this reason, the divine Chrysostom, following the sacred Canons of the Holy Apostles and of the sacred Council which we previously mentioned, and certainly considering how all of the sacred rituals of the Divine Liturgy look to the Communion of the faithful, judges those people who go to the Liturgy and do not commune to be unworthy even of entering into the Church:

> I observe many partaking of Christ's body lightly and haphazardly, and rather from custom and form than from consideration and understanding. "When," says someone, "the season of Holy Lent sets in," whatever kind of person he may be, he partakes of the Mysteries, or, when the day of Theophany comes. And yet it is not Epiphany nor is it Lent that makes someone worthy of approaching, but it is sincerity and purity of soul. With this, approach at all times; without it, never. "For as often," the Apostle says, "as ye do this, ye proclaim the Lord's death" (1 Cor. 11:26), that is to say, "you make a remembrance of the salvation that has been wrought for you, and of the benefits which I have bestowed." Consider those who partook of the sacrifice under the Old Covenant, what great abstinence did they not practice! How did they not conduct themselves! What did they not perform! They were always purifying themselves. And do you, when you draw nigh to the Sacrifice, at which the very angels tremble, do you measure the matter by the revolutions of the seasons? And how will you present yourself before the judgment-seat of Christ, you who presume upon His body with polluted hands and lips?

> …Observe the vast inconsistency of the thing. At the other times you do not come, no—not that you are often clean. But at Pascha, however flagrant an act you may have committed, you come. O the force of custom and of prejudice! In vain is the daily Sacrifice. In vain do we stand before the altar: there is no one to partake. These things I am saying, not to induce you simply to partake, but that you should render yourselves worthy to partake.

Are you not worthy of the Sacrifice, or of receiving it? If so, then neither are you of the prayers. You hear the herald (the deacon, that is), standing, and saying: "As many as are in penitence, all pray." As many as do not partake, are in penitence. If you are one of those that are in penitence, you ought not to partake; for he that does not partake is one of those that are in penitence. Why then when he says: "Depart, you that are not qualified to pray," do you have the audacity to stand still? But no, you are not of that number, you are of the number of those who are able to partake, and yet you are indifferent about it and regard the matter as nothing.

Look, I entreat. A royal Table is set before you, angels minister at that Table, the King Himself is there, and do you stand gaping? Are your garments defiled, and yet you make no account of it? Or are they clean? Then fall down and partake. Every day He comes in to see the guests, and converses with them all. Yes, at this moment is He speaking to your conscience: "Friend, how do you stand here, not having on a wedding garment?" He did not say: "Why did you sit down?" No, before the man sat down and before he even entered the feast, He declared him to be unworthy. He does not say: "Why did you sit down to eat,' "but: "Why did you come in?" And these are the words that He is at this very moment addressing to one and all of us who stand here with such shameless audacity. For everyone that does not partake of the Mysteries is standing here in shameless audacity. It is for this reason that they which are in sins are first of all put out of the Church.

For, when a master is present at his table, it is not right that those servants who have offended him should be present; but rather they are sent out. Just so here, when the Sacrifice of the Lamb is brought forth, and Christ, the Master's Sheep, is sacrificed, when you hear the words: "Let us pray together," when you behold the curtains drawn up, then imagine that the heavens are let down from above, and that the angels are descending! As it is not then right that any one of the uninitiated should be present, so neither should be present one of them who, though initiated, are at the same time defiled.

Tell me, suppose someone was invited to a feast, and was to wash his hands, and sit down, and be all ready at the table, and after all that, refuse to partake. Is he not insulting the man who invited him? Were it not better for such a person never to have come at all? Now it is in just the same way that you have come here. You have sung the hymn with the rest: you have declared yourself to be of the number of them that are worthy by not departing with them that are unworthy. Why stay, and yet not partake of the Table? "I am unworthy," you will say. Then you are also unworthy of that communion you have had in the prayers. For it is not by means of the offerings only, but also by means of those songs that the Spirit descends all around. Do we not see our own servants first scouring the table with a sponge, cleaning the house, and then setting out the entertainment? This is what is done by the prayers, by the cry of the herald. We scour the Church, as it were, with a sponge, that all things may be set out in a pure Church, that there may be "neither spot nor wrinkle" (Eph. 5:27). Unworthy, indeed, are our eyes of these sights, and unworthy our ears! "And if even a beast," it is said, "touch the mountain, it shall be stoned" (Ex. 19:13). Thus then they were not worthy so much as to set foot on it, but afterwards they came near and beheld where God had stood. And you may, afterwards, come near and behold; however, when He is present, depart. You are no more allowed to be here than the catechumen is. For indeed, to have never reached the Mysteries is not at all the same thing, as, when you have reached them, to stumble before them and despise them, and to make yourself unworthy of this.

One might enter upon more points, and those more awful still. However, not to burden your understanding, these will suffice. They who are not brought to their right senses with these, certainly will not be with more. That I may not then be the means of increasing your condemnation, I entreat you not to forbear coming, but to render yourselves worthy both of being present and of approaching. Tell me, were any king to give command and say: "If any man does this, let him partake of my table," would you not do all you could to be admitted? He has invited us to heaven, to the Table of the great and wonderful King, and do we shrink and hesitate, instead of hastening and running to it? And what then is our hope of salvation? We cannot lay the blame on our weakness; we cannot lay it on our nature. It is indolence and nothing else that renders us unworthy.[93]

Do your hear, my brother, what this great teacher of the Church says? That those who are not prepared to receive Communion (though they do not have an impediment) are not even worthy to attend the Divine Liturgy.

But how do you respond? You say: "If this is how things are, then I just won't go to Liturgy at all."

No, my brother, no. You are not even allowed to do this, for you will be excommunicated, as the Holy and Sixth (Quinisext) Ecumenical Council decrees: "If anyone… being in town does not go to Church on three consecutive Sundays—that is, three weeks— if he is a cleric let him be deposed, but if he is a layman, let him be cut off from Communion."[94] This is also decreed by the eleventh Canon of the Holy and sacred Local Council in Sardica.[95]

So then, beloved, you are subject to the penance of excommunication if you do not do both things, namely, attend the Liturgy, and prepare yourself, as much as possible, to receive

---

93 *On Ephesians* 3, 4–5, PG 62, 28–30; NPNF (V1-13), 63–65.

94 Canon 80 (*Pedalion*, 290; *The Rudder*, 384).

95 Cf. *Pedalion*, 454; *The Rudder*, 592.

Communion if you do not have an impediment. You cannot transgress either the one or the other.

By doing this, you are observing all of the sacred rituals of the Divine Liturgy, as we said previously, and you do not transgress the order which the Church received from our very Lord, from the Apostles, from the Councils, and from the Saints. And this is the order: for the Holy Bread to be divided at every Divine Liturgy, and for the faithful (that is, the faithful who do not have an impediment) to partake of it.

This is what Symeon of Thessaloniki says: "The Divine Liturgy is a rite during which the all-holy body and blood of Christ itself is consecrated and then given to all of the faithful in Communion, and Communion is the sole purpose of the Divine Liturgy."[96]

The sacred Bishop of Dyrrachios, Nicholas Cabasilas, writes: "The work of the Holy Rite of the sacred Mysteries is the change of the divine Gifts into the divine body and blood; and its purpose is for the faithful to be sanctified through them."[97]

The wise Job (to whom the sacred Photios bears witness in his *Myriobiblon* or *Bibliotheca*) says in the work *On the Mysteries* that "the entire Divine Liturgy signifies and points to the Communion of the Mysteries, for this is its aim, purpose, and work, namely, for the faithful to receive the life-giving and dread Mysteries."[98]

Gabriel of Philadelphia, in the work entitled *On the Mysteries*, says that the Divine Liturgy takes place for three reasons. First, unto the glory and praise of our God and Savior, and unto the remembrance of His death and resurrection, just as He said: "This do in remembrance of Me" (Lk. 22:19). Second, for the repose and sanctification of the souls of pious Orthodox Christians

---

96 Cf. *De Sacra Liturgia*, ch. 99, PG 155, 300B.

97 *Sacrae Liturgiae Interpretatio* 1, PG 150, 368–369A; *A Commentary on the Divine Liturgy* (Crestwood: St. Vladimir's Seminary Press, 1998), 25. [Translator's note: Bishop Nicholas of Methone writes: "The purpose of the rite is to participate in Christ and to receive life eternal. That is to say, it is for the deification of the participants" (*De Corpore et Sanguine Christi*, PG 135, 512B).]

98 See the *Syntagmation* of Chrysanthos of Jerusalem (Tyrgobist: 1715).

who have fallen asleep.[99] And, third, for the living.[100] Wherefore, when the Divine Liturgy is celebrated unto the glory, praise, and remembrance of the death and resurrection of our Lord, our brothers who have fallen asleep in the faith receive, as much as possible, rest and sanctification from God. But concerning the living faithful who do not receive the divine Mysteries during the Liturgy, I am in wonder and don't know how they can be sanctified at all. The sacred Cabasilas says that they are not sanctified. Listen:

> If then those living souls are ready and prepared for the Mystery, and if the Lord Who sanctifies and perfects wishes to sanctify, and desires to continue to give Himself, what can prevent such a communion? Certainly nothing. Then someone will say, if one among the living has the aforementioned good qualities in his soul, but does not approach the Mysteries, will he nevertheless receive the sanctification which they give? Not in all cases, but only if someone cannot physically approach, as it is for the souls of the dead.... If, however, someone is able to approach the Table, but does not, it is impossible for him to receive the sanctification which the Mysteries bring; not just because he did not approach, but because, being able, he did not.[101]

4. Not only does everything which we have said up until now obligate every Christian that does not have an impediment to receive Communion frequently, but even divine Communion in and of itself, if we think about it, beckons each person to partake of it frequently simply because it is a constituent of the life of the soul. Let us see, however, what this means.

The scholastic theologians call Communion constitutive, because "the constitutive" is that without which it is impossible

---

99 Cf. Augustine of Hippo, *Enchiridion de Fide, Spe et Charitate* 110, PL 40, 283 (NPNF [V1-03], 272), and Nicholas Cabasilas, *Sacrae Liturgiae Interpretatio* 42, PG 150, 457B-460C (*A Commentary on the Divine Liturgy*, 96-98).

100 *Syntagmation Peri ton Hagion kai Hieron Mysterion* (Venice: 1591).

101 *Sacrae Liturgiae Interpretatio* 42, PG 150, 457D–460A; *A Commentary on the Divine Liturgy*, 97.

for something that happens to happen. For example, breath is constitutive to the life of man, for, without it, man cannot live. And food is necessary for the constitution of the body. Now, just as frequent breathing is necessary for life and food is necessary for the constitution of the nature of the body, in like manner is frequent Communion necessary for the life of the soul and for the constitution of its essence; or, rather, it is incomparably more necessary.

Now let Basil the Great, that foundation of the right dogmas of the Church, come onto the scene and speak to us. He says: "The receiving of the body and blood of Christ is necessary for eternal life."[102] And, again, he says: "He who has been reborn through Baptism must now be nourished by partaking of the divine Mysteries…. Therefore, we are now nourished with the food of eternal life, which the Son of the living God handed down to us."[103] And again, when asked a question by a patrician woman named Caesarea, he replied to her in an epistle saying: "It is good and beneficial to commune every day, and to partake of the holy body and blood of Christ, Who clearly says: 'Whoso eateth My flesh, and drinketh My blood, hath eternal life' (Jn. 6:54). For who doubts that to frequently participate in life is nothing other than to have manifold life?"[104] In other words, who doubts that to receive Communion frequently is to live in many ways, that is, to live with all of the powers and senses of the soul and body?

The monk Job the Confessor says:

> It is just and right for the Christian to be sanctified frequently and many times by receiving divine Communion, and he

---

102 *Moralia* 21, PG 31, 816C; *Saint Basil: Ascetical Works*, 101.

103 *De Baptismo* 1.3, PG 31, 1573A; *Saint Basil: Ascetical Works*, 386, 387.

104 *Epistola* 93, PG 32, 484B; NPNF (V2-08), 179. [Translator's note: St. Basil the Great is not alone in interpreting these words of the Savior from the sixth chapter of the Gospel according to John as referring to the Holy Eucharist. Countless other Fathers of the Church do so as well; for example, Cyprian of Carthage, Ambrose of Milan, John Chrysostom, Cyril of Alexandria, Augustine of Hippo, John of Damaskos, Symeon the New Theologian, Gregory Palamas, Nicholas Cabasilas, and Symeon of Thessaloniki—to name but a few. Moreover, the Divine Liturgy of the Presanctified Gifts also interprets these words of Christ as referring to Holy Communion.]

should run to it more often, and desire to commune more than he desires to breathe. For this reason, each person has permission to receive Communion frequently, and, if it is possible, those who are worthy are not prohibited to commune every day.[105]

Patriarch Gennadios of Constantinople most wisely depicts how necessary Holy Communion is for the Christian, saying:

And now the Mystery brings about in those who partake of it progress in the life according to Christ. For the effects it produces physically (that is, in that the bread and wine nourish the body), it produces in an analogous way inwardly, mystically and invisibly. For the body of Christ nourishes and refreshes our soul, just as bread does the body. And just as we were reborn through Baptism and received the existence of grace in the place of the existence of sin, so by being nourished with the Mystery of Communion we are strengthened, and we remain and progress in grace. The natural heat of the body can dry out its natural hydration if the body is not aided by food. (For this reason the composition of the body must be preserved by food and drink, and the fluids which were lost on account of heat replenished. It is impossible for human life to be sustained even for a short while in any other way). In like manner, the heat of evil, which gnaws away at the soul by drying out the quality of piety, would certainly destroy it completely if the soul did not receive spiritual food, which thwarts the corrupting power of evil and renews and increases the spiritual gifts of God within us. The body of Christ, since it nourishes the body, and since it is united to the Divine Nature, purifies and sanctifies those who receive Communion, and grants to us sufficient spiritual nourishment. Thus, with this food we are well nourished and receive our spiritual purity and

---

105 See the *Syntagmation* of Chrysanthos.

health, from which Paradisiacal health the tasting of the forbidden tree removed us.

We, then, who lost that original purity and health through bodily food, must regain it through bodily food, thus treating like with like, and opposites with opposites. That is, it was bodily food that ruined us in Paradise; and Communion is also bodily food, but which preserves us. Likewise, both health and spiritual life were corrupted then, but are now preserved. And, though then God prevented us from eating the food, now He gives us the food and urges us towards it. And the evil demon taught us regarding that food, but, concerning this food, not only is the Son of God the Counselor, but He Himself serves it. Moreover, that food was stolen by us, but we are openly called to receive this food. Further, in that food was hidden the poison of transgression, but in this food is hidden a treasury of innumerable blessings.[106]

So, my brothers, since we have demonstrated from these testimonies that frequent Communion is necessary for those Christians (who do not have an impediment), we also, then, have a great need to commune frequently, so that we can have life, which is Jesus Christ, in ourselves, and so that we do not die a spiritual death. For as many as are not frequently nourished by that spiritual food will most surely die. Even if it appears that they are physically alive, they are spiritually dead, because they have distanced themselves from the spiritual and true life brought about by Holy Communion.

When an infant is first born, it cries and eagerly looks for food and milk. If it does not nurse, it does not have an appetite, and this is a sign that it is sick and is in danger of death. We also must eagerly want to be nursed by the spiritual food of Holy Communion, in order to be given life. Otherwise we are in danger of dying spiritually.

For this reason, the divine Chrysostom says:

---

106 See the *Syntagmation* of Chrysanthos; *De Sacramentali Corpore Christi* 1, PG 160, 356B–357A.

Let us not then be negligent, having been deemed worthy of such love and honor (to receive Christ's body and blood, that is). Do you not see with how much eagerness infants lay hold of the breast? With what earnest desire they fix their lips upon the nipple? With such eagerness and desire let us also approach this Table and the nipple of the spiritual Cup. Or, rather, with much greater eagerness, let us like nursing infants draw out the grace of the Spirit, and let only one thing be our sorrow—not to partake of this Food.[107]

CHAPTER 2

Frequent Reception of the Holy Mysteries is Beneficial and Salvific

Both the soul and the body of the Christian receive great benefit from the divine Mysteries—before he communes, when he communes, and after he communes. Before one communes, he must perform the necessary preparation, namely, confess to his Spiritual Father, have contrition, amend his ways, have compunction, learn to watch over himself carefully, and keep himself from passionate thoughts (as much as possible) and from every evil. The more the Christian practices self-control, prays, and keeps vigil, the more pious he becomes and the more he performs every other good work, contemplating what a fearful King he will receive inside of himself. This is even more true when he considers that he will receive grace from Holy Communion in proportion to his preparation. The more often someone prepares himself, the more benefit he receives.[108]

---

107 *On Matthew* 82.5, PG 58, 744; NPNF (V1-10), 476-477.

108 Translator's note: Interpreting the Third Ode of the Canon of the Feast of the Elevation of the Cross, St. Nikodemos writes:

> So, my beloved reader, if you desire to receive the abovementioned divine charismata [forgiveness of sins, enlightenment, justification, sanctification, victory over the devil, etc], and still others even more unspeakable and incomprehensible, frequently approach the immaculate Mysteries and partake of them. Take care, however, to receive Communion with the appropriate preparation, namely, with confession, with fasting (as much as you

When a Christian partakes of Communion, who can comprehend the gifts and the charismata he receives? Or how can our inept tongue enumerate them? For this reason, let us again bring forward one by one the sacred teachers of the Church to tell us about these gifts, with their eloquent and God-inspired mouths.

Gregory the Theologian says:

> When the most sacred body of Christ is received and eaten in a proper manner, it becomes a weapon against those who war against us, it returns to God those who had left Him, it strengthens the weak, it causes the healthy to be glad, it heals sicknesses, and it preserves health. Through it we become meek and more willing to accept correction, more longsuffering in our pains, more fervent in our love, more detailed in our knowledge, more willing to do obedience, and keener in the workings of the charismata of the Spirit. But all the opposite happens to those who do not receive Communion in a proper manner.[109]

Those who do not receive Communion frequently suffer totally opposite things, because they are not sealed with the precious blood of our Lord, as the same Gregory the Theologian says: "Then the Lamb is slain, and with the precious blood are sealed action and reason, that is, habit and mental activity, the sideposts of our doors. I mean, of course, by 'doors,' the movements and notions of the

---

are able), with the preparation of self-control, with prayer, with attentive care, with contrition in your heart, and with a pure conscience, having examined yourself just as the Apostle commands you (cf. 1 Cor. 11:28), so that your partaking of the divine Mysteries not be unto your condemnation. You will receive the grace of Communion in proportion to the extent of your preparation for receiving it. You must therefore do two things: you must commune frequently, and you must commune worthily, as much as this is possible (barring any impediment designated by the sacred Canons)" (*Heortodromion* [*Festal Guide*]. vol. 1 [Thessaloniki: Orthodoxos Kypsele, 1987], 68–69).

109 Translator's note: This quote is taken from Gennadios Scholarios (*De Sacramentali Corpore Christi* 1, PG 160, 357A), who himself says he is quoting "the divine Gregory."

intellect, which are opened and closed correctly through spiritual vision."[110]

St. Ephraim the Syrian writes:

> Brothers, let us practice stillness, fasting, prayer, and tears; gather together in the Church; work with our hands; speak about the Holy Fathers; be obedient to the truth; and listen to the divine Scriptures; so that our minds do not become barren (and sprout the thorns of evil thoughts). And let us certainly make ourselves worthy of partaking of the divine and immaculate Mysteries, so that our soul may be purified from thoughts of unbelief and impurity, and so that the Lord will dwell within us and deliver us from the evil one.

The divine Cyril of Alexandria says that, because of divine Communion, those noetic thieves the demons find no opportunity to enter into our souls through the senses:

> You must consider your senses as the door to a house. Through the senses all images of things enter into the heart, and, through the senses, the innumerable multitude of lusts pour into it. The Prophet Joel calls the senses windows, saying: "They shall enter in at our windows like a thief" (Jl. 2:9), because these windows have not been marked with the precious blood of Christ. Moreover, the Law commanded that, after the slaughter (of the lamb), the Israelites were to smear the doorposts and the lintels of their houses with its blood, showing by this that the precious blood of Christ protects our own earthly dwelling-place, which is to say, our body, and that the death brought about by the transgression is repelled through our enjoyment of the partaking of life (that is, of life-giving Communion). Further, through our sealing (with the blood of Christ) we distance from ourselves the destroyer.[111]

---

110 *Oratio* 45.15, PG 36, 644B; NPNF (V2-07), 428.
111 *Glaphyra in Exodum* 2.2, PG 69, 428B.

The same divine Cyril says in another place that, through Communion, we are cleansed from every impurity of soul and receive eagerness and fervor to do good: "The precious blood of Christ not only frees us from every corruption, but it also cleanses us from every impurity lying hidden within us, and it does not allow us to grow cold on account of sloth, but rather makes us fervent in the Spirit."[112]

St. Theodore the Studite wondrously describes the benefit one receives from frequent Communion:

> Tears and contrition have great power. But the Communion of the sanctified Gifts, above all, has especially great power and benefit, and, seeing that you are so indifferent towards it and do not frequently receive it, I am in wonder and great amazement. For I see that you only receive Communion on Sundays, but, if there is a Liturgy on any other day, you do not commune, though when I was in the monastery each one of you had permission to commune every day, if you so desired. But now the Liturgy is less frequently celebrated, and you still do not commune. I say these things to you, not because I wish for you simply to commune—haphazardly, without preparation (for it is written: "But let a man examine himself, and so let him eat of the Bread, and drink of the Cup. For he that eateth and drinketh unworthily, eateth and drinketh damnation to himself, not discerning the Lord's body and blood" [1 Cor. 11:28–29]). No, I am not saying this. God forbid! I say that we should, out of our desire for Communion, purify ourselves as much as possible and make ourselves worthy of the Gift. For the Bread which came down from heaven is participation in life: "If any man eat of this bread, he shall live for ever: and the bread that I will give is My flesh, which I will give for the life of the world" (Jn. 6:51). Again He says: "He that eateth My flesh, and drinketh My blood, dwelleth in Me, and I in him" (Jn. 6:58).

---

112 *De Adoratione et Cultu in Spiritu et Veritate* 17, PG 68, 1077D.

Do you see the ineffable gift? He not only died for us, but He also gives Himself to us as food. What could show more love than this? What is more salvific to the soul? Moreover, no one fails to partake every day of the food and drink of the common table. And, if it happens that someone does not eat, he becomes greatly dismayed. And we are not speaking here about ordinary bread, but about the Bread of life; not about an ordinary cup, but about the Cup of immortality. And do we consider Communion an indifferent matter, entirely unnecessary? How is this thought not irrational and foolish? If this is how it has been up until now, my children, I ask that we henceforth take heed to ourselves, and, knowing the power of the Gift, let us purify ourselves as much as possible and partake of the sanctified Things. And if it happens that we are occupied with a handicraft, as soon as we hear the sounding-board calling us to Church, let us put our work aside and go partake of the Gift with great desire. And this (that is, frequent Communion) will certainly benefit us, for we keep ourselves pure through our preparation for Communion. If we do not commune frequently, it is impossible for us not to become subject to the passions. Frequent Communion will become for us a companion unto eternal life.[113]

So, my brothers, if we practice what the divine Fathers have ordered and frequently commune, we not only will have the support and help of divine grace in this short life, but also will have the angels of God as helpers, and the very Master of the angels Himself. Furthermore, the inimical demons will be greatly distanced from us, as the divine Chrysostom says:

Let us then return from that Table like lions breathing fire, having become fearsome to the devil, thinking about our Head (Christ) and the love He has shown for us.... This blood causes the image of our King to be fresh within us, it

---

113 *Small Catechesis* 107 (*Mikra Katechesis* [Thessaloniki: Orthodoxos Kypsele, 1984], 271–272)

produces unspeakable beauty, and, watering and nourishing our soul frequently, it does not permit its nobility to waste away…. This blood, worthily received, drives away demons and keeps them far from us, while it calls to us the angels and the Master of angels. For wherever they see the Master's blood, devils flee and angels run to gather together…. This blood is the salvation of our souls. By it the soul is washed, is made beautiful, and is inflamed; and it causes our intellect to be brighter than fire and makes the soul gleam more than gold…. Those who partake of this blood stand with the angels and the powers that are above, clothed in the kingly robe itself, armed with spiritual weapons. But I have not yet said anything great by this: for they are clothed even with the King Himself.[114]

Do you see, my beloved brother, how many wonderful charismata you receive if you frequently commune? Do you see that with frequent Communion the intellect is illumined, the mind is made to shine, and all of the powers of the soul are purified? If you also desire to kill the passions of the flesh, go to Communion frequently and you will succeed. Cyril of Alexandria confirms this for us: "Receive Holy Communion believing that it liberates us not only from death, but also from every illness. And this is because, when Christ dwells within us through frequent Communion, He pacifies and calms the fierce war of the flesh, ignites piety toward God, and deadens the passions."[115]

Thus, without frequent Communion we cannot be freed from the passions and ascend to the heights of dispassion; just as the Israelites, if they had not eaten the passover in Egypt, would not have been able to be freed. For "Egypt" means an impassioned life, and if we do not frequently receive the precious body and blood of our Lord (every day if it be possible), we will not be able to be freed from the noetic Pharaonians (that is, the passions and the demons). According to Cyril of Alexandria,

---

114 *On John* 46.3–4, PG 59, 260–262; NPNF (V1-14), 164–165.
115 *In Joannis Evangelium* 4.2, PG 73, 585A.

As long as those of Israel were slaves to the Egyptians, they slaughtered the lamb and ate the passover. This shows that the soul of man cannot be freed from the tyranny of the devil by any other means except the partaking of Christ. For He Himself says: "If the Son therefore shall make you free, ye shall be free indeed" (Jn. 8:36).[116]

Again St. Cyril says, "They had to sacrifice the lamb, being that it was a type of Christ, for they could not have been freed by any other means."[117]

So if we also desire to flee Egypt, namely, dark and oppressive sin, and to flee Pharaoh, that is, the noetic tyrant (according to Gregory the Theologian),[118] and inherit the land of the heart and the promise, we must have as our general (as the Israelites had Joshua [Jesus] the son of Nun as their general) our Lord Jesus Christ through the frequent reception of Communion. This way we will be able to conquer the Canaanites and the strangers, which are the disruptive passions of the flesh, and the Gibeonites, which are deceptive thoughts, in order that we may be able to remain in Jerusalem, which is interpreted "sacred peace" (as opposed to the peace of the world), as our Lord says: "My peace I give unto you: not as the world giveth, give I unto you" (Jn. 14:27). That is to say, "My own peace I give to you, O my disciples, the sacred and holy peace, not the peace which is of the world, which oftentimes looks also to wickedness."

Remaining in that sacred peace, we will be deemed worthy to receive inside our heart the promise of the Spirit, just as the Apostles remained and waited in Jerusalem, according to the command of the Lord, and received the perfection and grace of the Spirit on the day of Pentecost. And peace is a charisma which attracts all of the other divine charismata; and the Lord dwells in peace, as the Prophet Elias says, for God was neither in the powerful and strong

---

116 *Glaphyra in Exodum* 2.2, PG 69, 421A–421B.

117 *De Adoratione et Cultu in Spiritu et Veritate* 1, PG 68, 205D.

118 Cf. *Oratio* 45.15, PG 36, 644A; NPNF (V2-07), 428..

wind, nor in the earthquake, nor in the fire, but in the gentle and peaceful breeze.[119]

However, without the other virtues, one cannot acquire peace. And virtue cannot be achieved without keeping the commandments. And no commandment is perfected without love, and love is not renewed without divine Communion. Wherefore, without divine Communion, we labor in vain.

Many obtain a variety of virtues on their own, thinking that they can be saved by these without frequent Communion, which is however fundamentally impossible. For they do not want to be obedient to the will of God and commune frequently, according to the norm of the Church, when they come together at every festive Liturgy.

To such people, God says through the Prophet Jeremiah: "They have forsaken Me, the fountain of living waters, and hewed them out cisterns, broken cisterns, that can hold no water" (Jer. 2:13). That is to say, "They left Me, God, Who is the fount of the life-giving water, namely, the virtue and charismata of the Holy Spirit, and they dug out for themselves wells full of holes, which cannot hold water." He again says through the Prophet Isaiah:

> Yet they seek Me daily, and delight to know My ways, as a nation that did righteousness, and forsook not the ordinance of their God. They ask of Me the ordinances of justice; they take delight in approaching to God. Wherefore have we fasted, say they, and Thou seest not? Wherefore have we afflicted our soul, and Thou takest no knowledge? Behold, in the day of your fast ye find pleasure, and exact all your labours. Behold, ye fast for strife and debate, and to smite with the fist of wickedness. Ye shall not fast as ye do this day, to make your voice to be heard on high. Is it such a fast that I have chosen? A day for a man to afflict his soul? Is it to bow down his head as a bulrush, and to spread sackcloth and ashes under him? Wilt thou call this a fast, and an acceptable day to the Lord? (Is. 58:2–5).

---

119 Cf. 3 Kg. [1 Kg.] 19:11–12.

That is, "They sought Me daily and desired to learn the wisdom of My providence, as if they were some righteous people which kept the ordinances of God. And they say: 'Lord, why did You not see us when we fasted? Why do You not want to know that we underwent such hardship?'" And God answers: "I do not hear you. For whenever you fast, you continue to do your wicked will. I do not want such a fast, nor such hardship. And even if you were to spread sackcloth and ashes on the ground beneath you like a bed, still I would not accept such a fast."

However, when labors and virtues are done according to the will of God, then are they acceptable to Him and beneficial. The will of God is that we do whatever our Lord commands, Who says to us: "Whoso eateth My flesh, and drinketh My blood, hath eternal life" (Jn. 6:54). This is not only a commandment, but the chief of all of the commandments, for it is constitutive of and perfects the rest of the commandments.

Wherefore, my beloved, if you desire to ignite in your heart divine eros and to acquire love for Christ, and with this love to acquire all the rest of the virtues, go regularly to Holy Communion. For it is impossible that someone will not love Christ, and be loved by Christ, when he frequently partakes of His holy body and blood. This is something natural, as we shall see.

Many wonder, why do parents love their children? And why do children love their parents in return? And we reply that no one has ever hated himself or his own body. Thus it is natural for children to love their parents, because their bodies come from the bodies of their parents, and they eat and are nourished by the blood of their mother both while in the womb and after they are born (for milk is naturally nothing other than blood which has become white). For these reasons, I say, it is a natural law for children to love their parents, and, likewise, for parents to love their children in return—because they were conceived from their own bodies. In the same way, as many as frequently receive the body and blood of our Lord will naturally rekindle their desire and love for Him. On the one hand, this is because as often as Christians partake of that life-flowing and life-giving body and blood, it warms them to love, even if they are the most thankless and hard-hearted of people. On the other hand, it is because the knowledge of our love for God is not something foreign to us, but is naturally sown in our heart from the moment that we are born according to the flesh, and when we are reborn according to the Spirit in Holy Baptism. At the slightest cause, those natural sparks immediately set ablaze, as the wise Basil says:

> Together with the making of the animal (I mean man), a certain seminal word was implanted in us, having within itself the tendency to impel us to love. The pupils in the school of God's commandments, having received this word, are by God's grace enabled to exercise it with care, to nourish it with knowledge, and to bring it to perfection.... You must know that this virtue, though only one, yet by its efficacy accomplishes and fulfills every commandment.[120]

In other words, when man was made, a certain power was immediately sown in him, which naturally generates love for God. The doing of the commandments of God diligently cultivates this power, nourishes it with knowledge, and perfects it by the grace of God. This virtue of love for God, though only one virtue, contains and activates all of the rest of the commandments.

This natural power to love God is strengthened, augmented, and perfected by the frequent Communion of the body and blood of our Lord. For this reason St. Cyprian writes that, when the martyrs were preparing to go off to their martyrdoms, they first partook of the immaculate Mysteries, and being thus strengthened by Holy Communion were set aflame with the love for God and went off to the stadium like lambs to the slaughter. And in return for the body and blood of Christ which they received, they shed their own blood and gave their body over to various tortures.

Is there any other good thing, O Christian, that you desire to have, which frequent Communion cannot give you? Do you desire to rejoice every day? Do you wish to celebrate brilliant Pascha

---

120 *Regulae Fusius* 2.1, PG 31, 908C; *Saint Basil: Ascetical Works*, 233.

whenever you like and to exult with unspeakable joy during this sorrowful life? Run frequently to the Mysteries and partake of them with the proper preparation and you will enjoy such things. For the true Pascha and the true festival of the soul is Christ, Who is sacrificed in the Mysteries as the Apostle says,[121] and as the divine Chrysostom likewise says:

> For Great Lent occurs but once a year. But we celebrate Pascha (that is, we receive Communion) three times a week or even four. Or, to say it better, as often as we like. For Pascha does not consist of fasting, but of the Offering and Sacrifice which takes place during the daily gathering. And as testimony that this is true, listen to Paul, who says: "Christ our passover [pascha] is sacrificed for us" (1 Cor. 5:7)…. Therefore, as often as you partake of Communion with a pure conscience, you celebrate Pascha; not when you fast, but when you partake of that Sacrifice…. The catechumen never celebrates Pascha, even though he may fast every year during Lent, because he does not commune in the Offering. So then, even the person who did not fast, if he approaches with a pure conscience, celebrates Pascha, be it today, tomorrow, or any time he partakes of Communion. For good and proper preparation for Communion is not judged by lengths of time, but by a pure conscience.[122]

Therefore, as many as fast for Pascha, but do not commune, do not celebrate Pascha, as the divine Father just told us. And as many as are not prepared to receive the body and blood of our Lord cannot truly celebrate Sundays or the other Feasts of the year, because they do not possess the cause and occasion for the Feast, which is the most-sweet Jesus Christ, and they do not possess the spiritual joy that divine Communion brings.

---

121 Cf. 1 Cor. 5:7.
122 *Adversus Judaeos* 3.4–5, PG 48, 867–868.

As many as think that Pascha and Feasts consist of abundant *artoklasies*,[123] bright candles, fragrant incense, and the silver and gold vessels that adorn the Church are deceived.[124] For God does not mainly seek such things from us, as He says through the Prophet Moses: "[O man], what doth the Lord thy God require of thee, but to fear the Lord thy God, to walk in all His ways, and to love Him, and to worship the Lord thy God with all thy heart and with all thy soul, to keep the commandments of the Lord, and His statutes" (Dt. 10:12–13).

Our concern now is not to discuss pious offerings made in Church and whether they are good or not. These, indeed, are good, but together with them we must also offer obedience to the holy commandments of our Lord, and to prefer this to all those things. According to the Prophet-king David: "A sacrifice unto God is a broken spirit; a heart that is broken and humbled God will not despise" (Ps. 50:17).

The Apostle Paul, in his Epistle to the Hebrews, says: "Sacrifice and offering Thou wouldest not, but a body hast Thou prepared me" (Heb. 10:5; Ps. 39:9). Which means: "O Lord, You do not desire that I bring to You all of the other sacrifices and offerings, but that I draw near to the Holy Mysteries and receive the all-holy body of Your Son, which You have prepared for me on the Holy Table, for this also is Your will." For this reason, wanting to show that he is ready to do obedience, the Psalmist says: "Then I said: Behold, I am come… to do Thy will, O my God, and Thy law is in the midst of my bowels" (Ps. 39:11; cf. Heb. 10:7). That is: "Behold Lord, I have come to do Your will with great eagerness and to fulfill Your law with all of my heart."

---

123 Translator's note: The *artoklasia* is a festive service conducted within Great Vespers, consisting of a procession, hymns, litanies, and the blessing of five loaves of bread together with wheat, wine, and oil.

124 Translator's note: Concerning this subject, see St. Symeon the New Theologian, *Ethical Discourses* 14, SC 129, 422–442; *On the Mystical Life*, vol. 1 (Crestwood: St. Vladimir's Seminary Press, 1995), 172–181.

For this reason, if we love our salvation, we must do the will of God and obey His commandments as sons and with joy, and not as slaves and with fear. For fear keeps the old commandments, while love keeps the evangelical commandments. That is, those who were under the Law kept the commandments and statutes of the Law out of fear, so they would not be disciplined and punished. But we Christians, since we are no longer under the Law, must do the commandments of the Gospel, not out of fear, but out of love, and we must do the will of God as sons.

The well-pleasing and ancient will of God the Father was to furnish His Only-begotten Son and our Lord Jesus Christ with a body, as the Apostle said.[125] That is, for His Son to become incarnate and shed His blood for the salvation of the world, and for all of us Christians to frequently partake of His body and His blood. Thus, we will be kept safe from the snares and machinations of the devil during this present life. And when our soul departs from us, it will fly like a dove in freedom and joy into the heavens, without being inhibited whatsoever by the spirits lurking in the air.

And this is verified by the divine Chrysostom, who says:

> Moreover another person told me (he says "another person" because he beforehand told of someone else, who had described to him a different vision)—not having heard it from someone else, but having himself been deemed worthy to both see and hear it—with regard to those who are about to depart this life, that if they happen to partake of the Mysteries, with a pure conscience, when they are about to breathe their last, angels keep guard over them because of what they have just received, and bear them hence (to heaven).[126]

So, my brother, because you do not know when death will come, whether today, or tomorrow, or this very hour, you must always be communed of the immaculate Mysteries in order to be found ready. And if it is the will of God that you continue to live this

---

125 Cf. Heb. 10:5–10.
126 *De Sacerdotio* 6.4, SC 272, 318; NPNF (V1-09), 76.

present life, you will live a life, by the grace of Holy Communion, full of joy, full of peace, and full of love, accompanied by all of the other virtues. But, if it is the will of God that you die, on account of Holy Communion you will pass freely through the tollhouses of the demons that are found in the air, and you will dwell with inexpressible joy in the eternal mansions.[127] For since you are always united to our sweet Jesus Christ, the almighty King, you will live a blessed life here; and, when you die, the demons will flee from you like lightning and the angels will open the heavenly entrance for you and usher you in procession to the throne of the blessed Trinity.[128]

O what majestic things Christians enjoy from frequent Communion, both in this present life and in the future life!

Would you like, O Christian, for the small errors you commit as a man, either with your eyes or with your ears, to be forgiven? Draw near to the Mysteries with fear and with a broken heart,[129] and they will be remitted and forgiven. St. Anastasios of Antioch confirms this:

> If we fall into some small, pardonable sins on account of our being human, either with our tongue, our ears, our eyes, and we fall as victims of deceit into vainglory, or sorrow, or anger, or some other like sin, let us condemn ourselves and confess to God. Thus let us partake of the Holy Mysteries, believing that the reception of the divine Mysteries is unto the purification of these small sins (though not the grave and evil and impure sins which we may have committed, regarding which we should seek the Mystery of Confession).[130]

Many other Saints also attest to this. The divine Clement of Rome says: "Having partaken of the precious body and precious

---

127 Cf. Jn. 14:2.

128 Translator's note: See St. Symeon of Thessaloniki, *De Ordine Sepulturae*, ch. 360, concerning the good of frequent Communion, especially its benefits at the hour of death (PG 155, 672B–673A).

129 Cf. Ps. 50:17.

130 Cf. *Quaestiones* 7, PG 89, 385C-389D.

blood of Christ, let us give thanks to Him who has deemed us worthy to partake of His Holy Mysteries, and ask that these may not be unto our condemnation, but unto our salvation... unto the forgiveness of sins."[131]

Basil the Great says: "And make them worthy to partake without condemnation of these, Thine immaculate and life-giving Mysteries, unto the forgiveness of sins."[132]

The divine Chrysostom says: "That to those who shall partake thereof they may be unto vigilance of soul, and unto forgiveness of sins."[133]

While confession and fulfilling one's ascetical rule is able to forgive sins, divine Communion is also necessary. One first removes the worms from a fetid wound, then cuts away the rotten skin, and finally applies ointment to it so that it may heal—for if it is left untreated, it reverts to its former condition—and the same is true in the case of sin. Confession removes the worms, fulfilling one's rule cuts away the dead skin, and divine Communion heals it as an ointment. For if divine Communion is not also applied, the poor sinner reverts to his former condition, "and the last state of that man becomes worse than the first" (Mt. 12:45).

Do you hear, my Christian, how many charismata you receive from frequent Communion? That your small, pardonable sins are forgiven and your wounds are treated and made completely well? What is more blessed than for you to always prepare yourself to receive Communion, and with the preparation for and the help of divine Communion always to find yourself free of sin? For you who are earthly to remain pure, as the heavenly angels are pure? Can there be any greater happiness than this?

And I will tell you something still greater, brother. If you frequently approach the Mysteries and partake worthily of that immortal and glorified body and blood of our Lord Jesus Christ, and become one body and one blood with the all-holy body and blood of Christ, the life-giving power and energy; then, at the

---

131 *Apostolic Constitutions*, Book 8, ch. 14, SC 336, 210; ANF (07), 491.

132 *Divine Liturgy of St. Basil the Great*, Prayer after the Lord's Prayer.

133 *Divine Liturgy of St. John Chrysostom*, Prayer after the sanctification of the Gifts.

resurrection of the righteous, your own body will be brought to life and resurrected incorruptible and glorified like that of Christ, as the divine Apostle writes to the Philippians: "Who shall change our lowly body, that it may be fashioned like unto His glorious body" (Phil. 3:21).

All of these great and supranatural dignities and graces of which we have spoken until now are received by every Christian who partakes of the divine Mysteries of our sweetest Jesus Christ with a pure conscience; and indeed even more than these are received, which we have not mentioned for the sake of brevity.

After one receives Communion, he thinks about the dread and heavenly Mysteries of which he partook, and so he takes heed to himself so as not to dishonor that grace. He fears his thoughts [*logismoi*], shrinks away from them, and protects himself from them. He begins a more correct and virtuous life, and, as much as is possible, abstains from every evil. When he begins to think about the fact that he will be receiving Communion again in just a few days, he doubles his efforts to watch over himself. He adds zeal to zeal, self-control to self-control, vigilance to vigilance, labors upon labors, and he struggles as much as possible. This is because he is pressed on two sides: on one side, because just a short while ago he received Communion, and on the other, because he will receive again in just a short while.

CHAPTER 3

Infrequent Communion Causes Great Harm

Infrequent Communion brings the complete opposite upon Christians. For whoever puts off receiving Communion does not perform a single preparation. He is not careful, and he does not guard himself from evil thoughts very well. This is because procrastination causes him to fall into negligence, and causes the warmth of piety and divine love to grow cold. The long period of abstinence gives him the opportunity to leisurely and carelessly walk through life, without having fear in his soul, without reining in his senses, and without watching carefully over his actions. But, rather, he allows himself to have total license with regard to food, words, and improper sights and sounds, and to become like a horse without a bridle, falling over every precipice of sin. All of these things indeed happen to those who put off receiving Communion, as we know from our own daily trial and experience.

I truly wonder how those who are worthy (as much as is possible, that is) to receive Communion, but put it off, are able to receive sanctification and grace from the divine Mysteries as Cabasilas described earlier. How can they extinguish the flame of the passions when they do not commune in the immaculate Mysteries, which according to the sacred Cyril drive away every illness, subdue the fierce war of the flesh, and deaden the passions?

How can they purify their intellects, enlighten their minds, or adorn any of the powers of their souls without partaking of the body and blood of our Lord, which according to the divine Chrysostom is the true purification, beauty, and enlightenment of the soul and its nobility, as we have read?

And how is it possible for them to flee the noetic Pharaoh, bitter Egypt, and dark sin, when they are not anointed and sealed with the precious blood of Christ, as Gregory the Theologian has described? And by what means can they ignite the flame of divine love in their hearts and receive spiritual joy, divine peace, and the other fruits and charismata of the Holy Spirit without receiving the body and blood of the Father's beloved Son, Who is of one essence with the Holy Spirit, and Who, according to the Apostle, is our true joy and peace and the fount of all good things?

I am bewildered and wonder over how today's Christians can celebrate Sundays and the other Feasts of the year and spiritually rejoice with true joy without frequently partaking of divine Communion, which is the reason and occasion for every Feast and celebration.

So, it is most certain that those who do not frequently commune are deprived (O, what a tragedy!) of all these heavenly and divine blessings. Furthermore, they are also transgressors of the commandments and of the decrees of the Lord, as we previously said, and of the Apostolic and Conciliar Canons, and of all of the teachings of the Saints which we have presented. And they are subject to the excommunication prescribed by the divine Apostles and the Council in Antioch, as we also have spoken about at length.

By procrastinating and not receiving Communion, such people also give the devil permission and opportunity to cast them into various sins and many other temptations, as the divine Cyril of Alexandria says: "Those who distance themselves from the Church and Communion become enemies of God and friends of the demons."[134]

In the words of the divine Chrysostom: "....that I may not, by long abstaining from Thy Communion, become prey to the noetic wolf."[135] That is: "For this reason, Lord, I frequently approach the Mysteries and partake, because I fear that, if I distance myself from Your Holy Communion for a long time, that noetic wolf, the devil, will find me bereft of Your grace and kill me."

The Righteous Palladios learned from Abba Makarios of Egypt that after he healed a certain woman (who by the workings of the devil appeared like a horse to the eyes of men) he gave her the following counsel: "You should never be absent from the Communion of the Mysteries of Christ, but should commune frequently, for this diabolic thing happened to you because you did not receive Communion for five weeks, and thus the devil found an opportunity to tempt you."[136]

---

134 *De exitu animi*, PG 77, 1088B.

135 Third Prayer before Holy Communion; trans. *A Prayer Book for Orthodox Christians*, 342. [Translator's note: In this same prayer, St. John Chrysostom also says that Holy Communion is a "defence against every operation of the devil" (Ibid., 341). And in the Seventh Prayer before Holy Communion, St. Symeon the New Theologian says that we must partake of the blameless Mysteries,

"Lest that foul deceiver find me,

All bereft of Thy divine grace,

And most guilefully seduce me,

And with scheming cunning lure me,

From Thy words which make me Godlike. (Ibid., 347–348)]

136 Cf. *Historia Lausiaca*, chs. 19, 20, PG 34, 1049A; *Palladius: The Lausiac History* (New York: Paulist Press, ACW, 1964), 56–57.

Likewise, on the day of his ordination, the divine Chrysostom healed a demoniac and admonished him to go to Church and receive the divine Mysteries frequently, with fasting and prayers,[137] so that the demon might not bother him again. This is written in the *Life* of St. John Chrysostom by Symeon Metaphrastes:

> A certain man who had an unclean demon suddenly jumped into the midst of the Church. Falling to the ground, he was foaming at the mouth with his tongue hanging out. All who were present witnessing such a sight fervently asked the holy and divine Chrysostom to supplicate God to heal the possessed man. The Saint told the man to come to him. As soon as he placed his hand upon him and called upon the Name of the Holy Trinity, looking upon him compassionately, he commanded the demon to come out of him. Immediately—O, what wonder!—his word took effect, and the man was straightway liberated from the terrible illness of the demon. After the Saint lifted him up off of the ground, he counseled him to attend Church, go to divine Communion, and to practice asceticism with fasting and prayer. He said: "If you live in this manner, you will never be bothered by the enemy again, nor will you be caught by the demonic traps and ambushes."

Do you hear, my brethren, what evils are suffered by those who do not frequently commune, but rather distance themselves from the Mysteries? Do you hear that they become possessed by demons and are changed into the likeness of irrational beasts, just like when of old king Nebuchadnezzar was changed into the likeness of an ox?[138] And they justly suffer these things. For they, although men, are able to become gods by grace by frequently partaking of divine Communion; and they do not want to, but keeping themselves from divine Communion, lose their human form and are changed into irrational beasts, and hand themselves over to the authority of Satan, as the Psalmist says: "For behold, they that remove themselves from

---

137 Cf. Mk. 9:29.
138 Cf. Dan. 4:33.

Thee shall perish" (Ps. 72:25). That is, "O Lord, behold, those who distance themselves from Your grace are completely lost."

If sudden death comes upon those who put off Communion and finds them unprepared, not having received the Mysteries, what will happen to these poor people? How will they be able to travel freely past those toll-collectors of the air, the demons? What fear and terror will their soul experience? And they would have been able to be freed of all these things through frequent Communion, as the divine Chrysostom said earlier. Be merciful, O God!

So, my brothers, since infrequent Communion brings us so many great and inexpressible evils, while frequent Communion grants us such lofty, great, heavenly, and supranatural good things, in both the present and future life, why do we delay so much to receive it? Why should we not prepare ourselves properly to commune in the divine Mysteries, if not daily, then every Saturday or Sunday and at every Feast? We should, with great joy, run frequently to the sacred Table to receive our sweetest Jesus Christ, our whole life and breath, our entire hope and salvation, so that we may always be united to and inseparable from Him, in both this life and the next. But, on the contrary, we are content as we are, and we take great joy in procrastinating and keeping ourselves away from Him.

If someone were to deprive us of the table of bodily foods for just one day, we would become sad and restless, and think it was something terrible. But if we are deprived of the spiritual and heavenly Table of the divine Mysteries for one or two days, for entire months, we do not consider it to be bad. What a great lack of discrimination today's Christians exercise regarding bodily things and spiritual ones! For they embrace the things of the body with all their love, yet do not at all desire the things of the spirit.

Many God-loving Christians expend a great deal of money, labor greatly, and endure many dangers, both by sea and by land, in order to go and venerate the Life-giving Tomb of the Lord in Jerusalem, and other holy places. And then they boast that they can call themselves "pilgrims" who have venerated at these sacred sites. Many who hear that there is to be found in a far away place a sacred relic of a certain Saint run with great eagerness to go and venerate it, in order to receive grace and sanctification.

But when it comes to partaking of the immaculate Mysteries and being deemed worthy to enjoy, not the Life-giving Tomb, not holy places, not relics of Saints, but the King of all and the Holy of Holies, they have scant desire, or it does not interest them at all. In order to visit the holy sites, much money must be spent, long roads must be traversed, and many dangers must be endured. On the other hand, in order to commune, money is not required, nor does one have to walk very far, nor does one have to undergo dangers. It is enough to make a contrite confession, fulfill a sound rule, and prepare properly, and immediately one can receive Communion and become one body and one blood with Christ. Yet, even with the ease of this, everyone is still negligent concerning Communion and declines it.[139]

Alas, my brothers! If we could but once see with the noetic eyes of our soul of what lofty and great blessings we are deprived by not frequently communing, then, indeed, we would do everything in our power to prepare ourselves to receive Communion, every day if it were possible.[140]

---

139 Translator's note: St. Nikodemos writes something very similar in his book, *Chrestoetheia ton Christianon* [*Christian Morality*]:

> I know that many of you Christians think it a great blessing and cause for boasting to go to Jerusalem and reverently and compunctionately venerate the holy pilgrimage sites there, namely, the Life-receiving Tomb of the Lord, holy Golgotha, sacred Bethlehem, and the rest. Many of you travel to far away places, toiling over land and sea, in order to piously venerate the sacred relics of many Saints…. Indeed, such a reverent pilgrimage and piety and journey is good and praiseworthy. But should you not have, brothers, if not greater piety, at least the same amount of piety and reverence, when you go to and attend the Church of Christ, where all of the pilgrimage sites found at Jerusalem are present symbolically? Should you not show the same compunction and good order and respect when you attend the dread and divine Liturgy at which you find present, not the relic of such and such a Saint, but the very life-giving and divine [*theoypostaton*] and wholly-undefiled body and blood of our Lord Jesus Christ, the Holy of Holies? (Homily 12.2 [Thessaloniki: Regopoulos, 1999], 315–316)

140 Translator's note: Commenting upon the Ninth Ode of the Canon of Great and Holy Thursday, St. Nikodemos exhorts us:

> Come, O faithful Christians, and having previously purified ourselves through the appropriate preparation—having confessed our sins, forgiven our enemies, and put

So, if we have displayed great negligence until now regarding Holy Communion, I ask with brotherly love from the bottom of my heart: from now on, let us awake from the deep slumber of sloth and acquire eagerness and diligence. And if someone possessing spiritual authority wishes to obstruct us from this virtuous work, let us not allow the fervor of our eagerness to grow cold right away. No. Rather, falling down, let us kiss his feet like the harlot[141] and persistently knock on the door seeking permission. I most certainly do not believe that there is to be found anyone so hard of heart that, seeing such fervent desire for Holy Communion, he would prohibit us. Rather, I am certain that, no matter how hard-hearted he may be, or how intimidated by the bad custom to which he has adhered until now, his heart will be inclined to permit us to fulfill our desire.

---

away all hate—and being adorned by a pure conscience, thus let us draw near to the divine Mysteries and enjoy the Master's hospitality; that is, let us enjoy the hospitality that the Master Christ prepares for us today, and the immortal and spiritual table set for those who are worthy. For He feeds us with His incorruptible and wholly-undefiled body, and He gives us to drink His incorruptible and life-giving blood. (*Heortodromion*, vol. 2 [1995], 165)

141 Cf. Lk. 7:37–38.

Work of Victor, 1660. Church of the Holy Unmercenaries, Naxos.

Christ the High Priest

I am that bread of life. Your fathers did eat manna in the wilderness, and are dead. This is the bread which cometh down from heaven, that a man may eat thereof and not die.

Jn. 6:48-50

PART THREE

OBJECTIONS – CLARIFICATIONS

OBJECTION 1

There are some pious men who, when they see a Christian communing frequently, and since they do not know the Scriptures, prevent him and reproach him. They tell him that frequent Communion is reserved for priests, and say: "If you want to commune frequently, then become a priest."

To such people we reply, not with our own words, but with the words of the Holy Scriptures, the sacred Councils, and the Saints and teachers of the Church. The priests' dignity is for them, as instruments, to offer and sanctify the divine Gifts through the descent of the Holy Spirit, and to intercede with God on behalf of the people. And there are other sacred rites which those who are not ordained cannot perform. I mean to say that, during Communion, when they receive the Mysteries, priests do not differ in any way from the laity or from monastics, except in this: that the priests impart Communion, while the laity receive it. And the priests receive Communion within the sanctuary, and directly, without the use of the sacred spoon, while the laity and monastics receive Communion outside of the sanctuary, and indirectly, from the sacred spoon.

That priests do not differ at all from the laity in regards to Communion, we have as a witness the divine Chrysostom, who says,

One Father begat us. We are all of the same birth pangs (that is, born from the same mother, the baptismal font). The same drink has been given to all, or rather, not only has the same drink been given, but also to drink from one Cup. For the Father, desiring to lead us to a kindly affection, has also devised this, that we should drink out of one Cup, which is a sign of extreme love.[142]

And elsewhere he says:

> But there are occasions on which there is no difference at all between the priest and those under him, for instance, when we are to partake of the dread Mysteries. For we are all alike deemed worthy of them, not as under the Old Covenant, when the priest ate some things and those under him other things, and it was not lawful for the people to partake of those things of which the priest partook. It is not so now, but one body and one Cup are set before all.[143]

Symeon of Thessaloniki says: "Communion is prepared for all of the faithful, and not just for the hierarch. Rather, the hierarch (or the priest) is to consecrate the all-holy body and blood of Christ and impart Communion to all of the faithful. All is done for the sake of Communion."[144]

Job the Sinner, in the work *On the Mysteries,* says: "The aim, purpose, and work (of the Divine Liturgy) is to partake of the life-giving, dread, and sanctified Mysteries. Wherefore, they are first given within the sanctuary to those who are ordained, and then they are given to the prepared faithful, who are without."[145]

It necessarily follows, then, that priests who liturgize must be the first to be prepared to commune, for they are the ones who make the offering. And then the people must be prepared, according to the Hieromartyr Clement: "Let the bishop commune first, then the presbyters, and the deacons, and the subdeacons, and the readers, and the chanters, and the ascetics, and the deaconesses, and the

---

142 *On Matthew* 32.7, PG 57, 386; NPNF (V1-10), 212-213.

143 *On 2 Corinthians* 18.3, PG 61, 527; NPNF (V1-12), 365-366.

144 Cf. *De Sacra Liturgia*, ch. 99, PG 155, 300B.

145 See the *Syntagmation* of Chrysanthos of Jerusalem.

virgins, and the widows, then the children, and then the rest of the faithful, according to order, with reverence and fear, without any disruptions."[146]

The aforementioned Job says further: "It is permissible for all alike to receive Communion daily, both priests and laity, men and children and the elderly, and every age and order of Christians."

Any priests who do not commune Christians who approach divine Communion with reverence and faith are judged as murderers by God, as it is written in the book of the Prophet Hosea: "The priests have hid the way, they have murdered the people of Shechem; for they have wrought iniquity among the people" (Hos. 6:9). That is, the priests have covered the way, and the will, and the commandments of God, rather than revealing them.

I am in wonder and am amazed if there really are such priests as this, who turn away those who approach the Mysteries—and who do not in the least consider that they are lying by their words. For these very same priests, towards the end of the Liturgy, call out with a loud voice inviting all of the faithful, saying: "With the fear of God, with faith, and with love, draw near." Namely, "Approach the Mysteries in order to partake of them." And then these very same ones deny their own words and turn away those who approach. I am at a loss to describe such disorder and confusion.

OBJECTION 2

Some object saying that we are supposed to commune only every forty days.

Those who raise this objection bring forward the testimony of the divine Chrysostom as a justification:

Why, then, do we fast for forty days? In the past, and especially at the time when Christ entrusted to us these Mysteries, many people approached without thought or preparation. Since the Fathers realized that it was harmful for a person to approach the Mysteries in this heedless fashion, they came together and marked out forty

---

146 *Apostolic Constitutions*, bk. 8, ch. 13, SC 336, 208, 210; ANF (07), 490.

days for people to fast, pray, and gather together to hear the word of God. Their purpose was that we might all scrupulously purify ourselves during this time by our prayers, almsgiving, fasting, vigils, tears, confession, and all the other pious practices, so that we might approach the Mysteries with our consciences purified as much as possible.[147]

To such people we reply that those who desire to support their arguments are accustomed to bringing forward sayings from the Holy Scripture or from one of the Saints, so that their hook may not be without bait, as the divine John Chrysostom says: "When a lie wishes to be convincing and to appear as true, it will not be believed if it does not first have a basis which appears as true."[148] This is exactly how these blessed people argue.

But one should not break and cut off the words of the divine Scripture, separating them from their context, and then use them in a twisted manner for his own purpose. For the divine Chrysostom also says,

> We must not just examine the saying in and of itself, but we must consider everything that follows it; for whom, by whom, and to whom it was said; and why, when, and how it was said. It is not sufficient for someone to say: "It is written in the Scriptures," nor can one simply and haphazardly separate words and cut them off from the rest of the body of the God-inspired Scriptures and from their context, and, thus receiving them barren and stripped from their relevant surroundings, boldly misconstrue them. In this way many corrupt dogmas of the devil have entered into our life, for the devil convinces the more careless to quote isolated sayings of the Holy Scriptures, or to add to or subtract from the Scriptures, thus hiding the truth.[149]

147 *Adversus Judaeos* 3.4, PG 48, 867.

148 Translator's note: This quote is actually from Bishop Severianos of Gabala (*De Mundi Creatione* 2.4, PG 56, 444). It is found among the works of Chrysostom (see PG 56, 429-430 nn). St. John of Damaskos quotes this exact saying in his *Parallela Rupefucaldina* (700.4, PG 96, 541A-541B), attributing it to Severianos.

149 *In illud: Domine, non est in Homine* 2, PG 56, 156.

It is for this reason that the objectors should not only say that "Chrysostom says" that the divine Fathers established the practice of fasting for forty days, and after that communing. On the contrary, they also must consider what precedes and what follows the passage in question, to see what the divine Father says in the same homily, and for what reason and to whom he preached it. For, in accordance with their assertions, they must also say that the divine Chrysostom made Holy Communion available only on the day of Pascha. If these "defenders of the forty days" wish to establish such a practice, they must, according to their own opinion, either commune only one time a year, that is, on the day of Pascha, and thus be like those people of whom the divine Chrysostom speaks; or they must have ten Lents a year, according to the number of times they are accustomed to commune.

If they do not agree to the first, and cannot succeed in the second, let them be silent and not criticize and misrepresent the divine Chrysostom. For they make him out to be opposed not only to the Apostles, the Ecumenical and Local Councils, and many other Godbearing Fathers who refer to frequent Communion, but also to himself, inasmuch as he writes more than the others concerning frequent Communion, in many of his homilies, including the one in question:

> So do not keep pleading this excuse, but show me that Christ did command us to do this. I am showing you quite the opposite. I am showing you that Christ not only did not command us to observe days but also even freed us from the obligation to do so. Hear what Paul had to say. And when I say Paul, I mean Christ; for it is Christ who moved Paul's soul to speak. What, then, did Paul say?
>
> "Ye observe days, and months, and times, and years. I am afraid of you, lest I have bestowed upon you labour in vain" (Gal. 4:10–11). And again: "For as often as ye eat this bread, and drink this cup, ye do shew the Lord's death" (1 Cor. 11:26). When he said: "As often as," Paul gave the right and power to decide this to those who approach the Mysteries,

and freed them from any obligation to observe days. Now our Pascha and Lent are not one and the same thing: the Pascha is one thing, Lent another. For Great Lent occurs but once a year. But we celebrate Pascha three times a week or even four. Or, to say it better, as often as we like. For Pascha does not consist of fasting, but of the Offering and Sacrifice which takes place during the daily gathering at the Liturgy. And as testimony that this is true, listen to Paul, who says: "Christ our passover (pascha) is sacrificed for us" (1 Cor. 5:7).... Therefore, as often as you partake of Communion with a pure conscience, you celebrate Pascha; not when you fast, but when you partake of that Sacrifice.... The catechumen never celebrates Pascha, even though he may fast every year during Lent, because he does not commune in the Offering. So then, even the person who did not fast, if he approaches with a pure conscience, celebrates Pascha, be it today, tomorrow, or any time he partakes of Communion. For good and proper preparation for Communion is not judged by lengths of time, but by a pure conscience.

Yet we do just the opposite. We fail to cleanse our mind and, even though we are burdened with ten thousand sins, we consider ourselves to have celebrated Pascha if we approached the Mysteries on that day. But this is certainly not the case. If you approach the altar on the very day of the Great and Holy Sabbath with an evil conscience, you fail to share in Communion and you leave without celebrating Pascha. But if you wash away your sins and commune today, you truly celebrate Pascha.

Therefore you must safeguard this exactness and vigor of spirit, not in the observance of the proper times but in your approaching the altar. Now you would elect to endure all things rather than change this custom. But rather, in like manner, you must disdain it and choose to do or suffer anything so as not to approach the Mysteries when you are burdened with sins.... You have grounds for shame if you do not change for the better but persist in your untimely contentiousness. That is what destroyed the Jews. While they were always wanting the old customs and life, these were stripped from them and they turned to impiety.[150]

And again St. Chrysostom says:

> I know that many of us, because of the custom of doing so during the Feast, will approach the divine Table. You must, however, as I have said so many times, not receive Communion just because of a certain Feast; but you must purify your conscience and then partake of the divine Table. For the sinner and unclean person is not worthy even during a Feast to partake of that holy and dread flesh. But the one who has washed away his sins through true repentance is clean, both during the Feast and at all times, and he is always worthy to partake of the divine Mysteries and enjoy the gifts and graces of God. I do not know why, but many overlook this. Such people, even if they are full of many sins, when they see that a Feast has arrived, rush because of the particular day and receive the sacred Mysteries, which they are not worthy even to look upon.[151]

Behold, then, that the divine Chrysostom not only clearly confirms his purpose and opinion to those who love to hear the truth, but also prophetically overturns that custom now observed by many, of communing only every forty days.

If one wanted to address the forty days, he would certainly report how extensive would be a catalogue of all that the divine Fathers wrote. We, however, will bring forth just a few things, so that the uncertain may be assured.

At the time of the Holy First Ecumenical Council, the Christians of Asia celebrated Pascha together with the Jews. As an excuse, they claimed that they had received this practice from John the Theologian and the Apostle Philip, and some others. Even though

---

150 *Adversus Judaeos* 3.4–5, PG 48, 866–869.

151 *De Baptismo Christi* 4, PG 49, 369–370.

many divine Fathers of various Local Councils wrote to them many times concerning this, they did not desist from their custom until the First Council convened. Among other things, this Council decreed that no one was any longer to celebrate Pascha with the Jews, but on the Sunday after the vernal equinox, so it would not fall on the same day as the Jewish Passover. Yet some persisted in their bad custom, and it is such people that the divine Chrysostom addressed his homily, reproving them for disregarding so many divine Fathers simply on account of bad custom.

For this reason he praises the dignity of the divine Fathers of the First Council and attributes to them the defining of Lent. He says that they established Lent, wanting to convince his hearers and bring them to obedience. For someone might not know that the fast of Holy Lent was established by the Holy Apostles, who say in their sixty-ninth Canon: "If a bishop, or presbyter, or deacon, or subdeacon, or reader, or chanter does not fast during Holy and Great Lent, or on Wednesdays and Fridays throughout the year, let him be deposed; if he is a layman, let him be excommunicated."[152]

Or, as St. Chrysostom says in another place, perhaps the Fathers of the First Council established Lent as it is known today, inasmuch as they added to it the Great and Holy Week of the Passion, for the following reason: "For this reason the Fathers lengthened the time of the fast, to give us time for repentance, and thus being purified to receive Communion."[153]

But the main reason the First Ecumenical Council established Lent, says the divine Chrysostom, appears to be the following. Since Christians of that time were negligent and some did not fast at all during Holy Lent, while some fasted for only three weeks, others fasted for six weeks, while still others did something else, each according to his local custom (as Socrates attests in his *Ecclesiastical History*),[154] the Fathers of the First Ecumenical Council renewed the Canon of the Holy Apostles and established that all were without fail to fast for the entirety of Lent. The divine Chrysostom says

---

152 *Pedalion*, 91; *The Rudder*, 122.
153 *In illud: Vidi Dominum* 6.3, SC 277, 218.
154 Cf. Book 5, ch. 22, PG 67, 625B–645A; NPNF (V2-02), 130-134.

that it was for the sake of this renewal that the Fathers formally delineated Lent, setting it down in writing.[155]

These objectors set up the divine Chrysostom as a defender of their forty- day custom. But since he himself tears down their ideas like a spider web, we will be silent and proceed to the other objections.

OBJECTION 3

Some object saying that the purpose of frequent Communion, according to the Fathers, is that we not completely spurn the Communion of the divine Mysteries, and that, if some people commune infrequently on account of their great fear and piety, approaching the Mysteries with greater reverence, they partake worthily.

We would ask the people who say these things to show us whence and from which witnesses they learned the intent of Christ and the Saints. Perhaps they ascended into the heavens like Paul and heard these things?[156] But Paul heard "unutterable utterances," which a man cannot repeat. So how are they able to repeat them? If they learned them from somewhere else, how is it that they are not found written in the books of our divine Fathers? If indeed they are written there, and we have not found them, we ask them please to show them to us.

In any case, the fear they claim should attend the reception of the Mysteries is not of God, as the Prophet says: "There have they feared with fear where no fear is" (Ps. 52:6). For fear should attend transgression of the commandments, but not compliant submission and obedience. And neither is their piety true, but rather fake and hypocritical, because true piety reverences the words and commandments of the Lord and does not violate them. And they say these things, not in order to make Christians more cautious and

---

155 Cf. *Adversus Judaeos* 3.4, PG 48, 867.
156 Cf. 2 Cor. 12:2–4.

reverent when it comes to Communion, but in order to discourage them and cut them off completely from it, and so bring them spiritual death.

For this reason, the divine Cyril of Alexandria replies to such supposedly pious people saying:

> And if we long for eternal life, if we pray to have the Giver of immortality in ourselves, let us neither like some of the more heedless refuse to be blessed (by not communing of the Mysteries, that is), nor let the devil who is deep in wickedness lay a perilous piety (towards the divine Mysteries) as a trap and snare for us. What do you reply to us? "Paul writes: 'For he that eateth and drinketh unworthily, eateth and drinketh damnation to himself' (1 Cor. 11:29). And I, having examined myself, see that I am not worthy." And so we reply to you: When then will you be worthy? When will you present yourself to Christ? For, if you are always going to be scared away by your mistakes, consider that, being human, you will never cease from making them ("As for transgressions, who can understand them?" [Ps. 18:12], says the Holy Psalmist), and you will be found completely without participation in that soul-saving sanctification (of the Mysteries).

> Decide then to lead a holier life, in harmony with the law and the commandments of God, and so partake of the blessing (of Communion), believing that it has power to expel, not only death, but also our illnesses. For Christ thus coming to be in us lulls the law which rages in the members of our flesh, kindles piety towards God, and mortifies the passions, not imputing to us the transgressions in which we lie, but rather healing us as ones sick. For, being the Good Shepherd that He is, He binds up the broken, He raises the fallen, and He lays down His life for His sheep.[157]

And again St. Cyril says:

---

157 *In Joannis Evangelium* 4.2, PG 73, 584D–585A.

The holy body of Christ then gives life to those who have it within them, and holds them together unto incorruption, being commingled with their bodies. For it is to be conceived of as the body of none other but Him Who is by nature life, having in itself the whole power of the united Word, and having the quality of, or rather fulfilled with, His effectuating energy, through which all things are given life and maintained in existence. But since all of this is so, let them who have now been baptized and have tasted the divine grace know that, if they go sluggishly or leisurely to Church and for a long time keep away from the blessing (of the Eucharist) through Christ, and put on a pernicious piety in that they will not mystically partake of Him, they exclude themselves from eternal life, in that they decline to be given life. And this their refusal, albeit perhaps seeming to be the fruit of piety, becomes a snare and a scandal. For they should rather labor with all of their strength and eagerness so that they may be resolute in clearing away sin, and should take care to live a life most comely, and so hasten with all boldness to partake of life…. For thus, shall we overcome the deceit of the devil and, having become "partakers of the Divine Nature" (2 Pet. 1:4), mount upward to life and incorruption.[158]

John Zonaras, in his interpretation of the second Canon of the Council in Antioch, says:

The Fathers use the word "shun" in this Canon, not to refer to cases in which someone actually hates Holy Communion, and for this reason does not commune, but rather to refer to the avoidance of Communion on account of supposed piety and humility. For if one were to actually spurn and avoid Holy Communion out of hate for it and as abhorring it, he would be condemned not only with excommunication but also with complete banishment and anathema.[159]

158 Ibid., 3.6, PG 73, 520D–521C.
159 PG 137, 1284A–1284B.

The divine Cyril and John Zonaras sufficiently rebuke the supposed piety of those who are negligent, a piety which does not bear beneficial and salvific fruit. On the contrary, this piety brings about death to the soul and total deprivation of eternal life. And eternal life is brought about through the frequent Communion of the divine Mysteries. All who are truly pious do not disregard the words of the Lord and the sacred Canons of the Apostles, Councils, and Saints, nor even think of doing so, fearing the judgment and condemnation that attend upon disobedience. Concerning these truly pious people, the Holy Spirit says through the Prophet Isaiah, "To such a man will I look, even to him that is meek, and humble, and peaceful, and trembleth at My words" (Is. 66:2).

OBJECTION 4

Some again put forth this opinion saying: "Look at the Righteous Mary of Egypt and many other hermits and ascetics who communed one time in their entire lives. This infrequency of partaking of Communion did not prevent them from being sanctified."

To these people we reply that hermits do not govern the Church, nor did the Church write the Canons for hermits, as the Apostle says: "The law is not made for a righteous man" (1 Tim. 1:9). And the divine Chrysostom adds:

> All those who had zeal for the philosophy and way of life of the New Covenant of the Gospel did not live this life on account of the fear of hell, or because they were threatened, or on account of punishment, but only on account of divine love and fervent desire for God. For they needed neither commands nor commandments and laws to urge them to love virtue and hate evil. But as noble children and free people, since they knew the nobility of their nature,

and without any sort of fear and punishment, they rushed towards virtue on their own accord.[160]

However, these same hermits, if they had the means to commune but did not, are also condemned as transgressors of the sacred Canons, and as disdainers of the divine Mysteries. But if they did not have the means to commune they are innocent, as the sacred Cabasilas says:

> If then those living souls are ready and prepared for the Mystery, and if the Lord Who sanctifies and perfects wishes to sanctify, and desires to continue to give Himself, what can prevent such a communion? Certainly nothing. Then, someone will say, if someone among the living has the aforementioned good qualities in his soul, but does not approach the Mysteries, will he nevertheless receive the sanctification which they give? Not everyone, but only if someone cannot physically approach, as it is for the souls of the dead, and as it was the case for those who lived in the deserts, and in the mountains, and in caves, and in holes in the earth, who were not near any altar and Church, nor was it possible for them to see a priest. Christ Himself invisibly sanctified them with this sanctification (of the Mysteries). We know this because they had life, which they could not have had without partaking of the Mystery, for Christ Himself said: "Except ye eat the flesh of the Son of Man and drink His blood, ye have no life in you" (Jn. 6:53). Another proof is the fact that God sent angels to several of these men with the Mystery. If, however, someone is able to approach the Table, but does not, it is impossible for him to receive the sanctification which they bring; not just because he did not approach, but, being able, he did not. And for this reason it shows that his soul is void of the good qualities required for the Mysteries. For what desire and eagerness for the Table does he possess who could easily come to it

---

160 *De Verbis Apostoli, Habentes Eumdem Spiritum* 1.6, PG 51, 286.

but will not? And what faith in God has he who does not fear the Lord's threatening words concerning those who despise this banquet? How can someone believe that that person actually loves the Mysteries which, although he is able to receive them, does not? For this reason it is not then surprising that Christ should grant to those souls that have departed from their bodies, and which are not guilty of any such evil, a share in that Table.[161]

OBJECTION 5

Some object saying that Holy Communion is something fearful. For this reason, a holy, angelic, and perfect life is required in order to commune.

That the Mystery of divine Communion is great and fearful, and that it requires a holy and pure life, no one doubts. For the mere word "holy" signifies a great deal. Only God is holy, for He has holiness by nature and not by acquisition. People who are deemed worthy of Holy Baptism receive holiness by participation in the Holy God. For this reason they are called holy ones (saints), because they received sanctification through the grace of the Holy Spirit in their rebirth from above. And furthermore, they are called holy because they partake of the holy body and blood of our Lord, always receiving sanctification from the divine Mysteries. And as much as they draw near to God by doing the Master's commandments, so much more are they sanctified, ascending towards perfection. On the contrary, as much as they distance themselves from God by neglecting the commandments, so much more are they deprived of sanctification and ruled by the passions, and so much more does evil increase in them. For evil is nothing other than deprivation of the good.[162]

---

161 *Sacrae Liturgiae Interpretatio* 42, PG 150, 457D–460C; *A Commentary on the Divine Liturgy*, 97-98.

162 Cf. Dionysios the Areopagite, *De Divinis Nominibus* 4.23 and 30, PG 3, 725C and 732B; *Pseudo-Dionysius: The Complete Works*, 91, 94.

Therefore, it is not at all prohibited to call as many as have been deemed worthy of the rebirth of the Holy Spirit "saints" and "holy." And it follows that they are in no way prohibited from frequently communing in the divine Gifts, being holy children by the grace of the Holy God. For this reason, the divine Chrysostom says that the Holy Things must be given to those who are saints and holy ones, and not to the unclean and polluted. To show what makes the saints different, he says:

> Let no sinner approach. However, I do not mean "no" sinner, because I would thus preclude myself above all from approaching the divine Table. What I mean is that no one who is persistently a sinner (that is, unconfessed and unrepentant) is to approach. For I know that we are all subject to penances because of our sins, and thàt no one can boast that he has a pure heart. That we do not have a pure heart, however, is not what is evil, but that we do not approach the One Who is able to purify us.[163]

Theodoret of Cyr says: "Of those who partake of the divine Mysteries, some partake as lambs, namely, those who are perfect in virtue; while others partake as goats, namely, those who have erased the stains of their sins through repentance."[164]

Therefore, even though the divine Fathers ascribe frequent Communion only to the perfect, it is clear that they do not seek perfection from communicants, but amendment of life through repentance. For just as all people are not of one and the same age in this visible world, so also are people at various stages in the spiritual world of the Church, according to the Parable of the Sower.[165] The perfect man offers God one hundred, the intermediate sixty, and the novice thirty, each according to his ability, and no one is rejected by God because he does not offer the hundred. And if we really

---

163 *In illud: Vidi Dominum* 6.3, SC 277, 220.

164 *Quaestiones in Exodum* 24, PG 80, 253B. [Translator's note: We read in the *Apostolic Constitutions*: "If any one be holy, let him draw near [to the Eucharist]; but if any one not be such, let him become so through repentance" (bk. 7, ch. 26, SC 336, 56; ANF [07], 470).]

165 Cf. Mt. 13:8.

think about it, we will see that it is impossible for anyone to arrive at perfection without frequent Communion of the Holy Mysteries, for without Communion love cannot be achieved; and, without love, obedience to the Master's commandments cannot be achieved either. For, as the wise Solomon says: "The beginning of wisdom is the most sincere desire for instruction, and concern for instruction is love of her, and love of her is the keeping of her laws, and giving heed to her laws is assurance of immortality, and immortality brings one near to God; so the desire for wisdom leads to the kingdom" (Wis. 6:17–20).

For this reason, the holy Abba Apollo, knowing that divine Communion is the perfection of divine love, numbers it with the commandment of love, saying that "upon these two commandments," namely, frequent Communion and love for one's neighbor, "hang the whole Law and the Prophets" (Mt. 22:40).[166]

But why should we say all of this? Do the people who raise the present objection commune every forty days as being perfect, or as being sinners and imperfect? If they commune as being perfect, they should commune more frequently, according to their own argument. But, if they commune as being imperfect, they must

---

166 Translator's note: This is demonstrated by the following words of Abba Apollo, found in Palladios' *Lausiac History*:

> We must bow down to our brothers when they approach. For we are not bowing down to them, but to God, as it is said: "When you see your brother, you see the Lord your God." This we have learned from Abraham (cf. Gen. 18). When you receive the brethren, invite them to rest for awhile, for this is what we learn from Lot, who so invited the angels (cf. Gen. 19:3). Also, the monks must commune of the Mysteries every day, if this is possible. For he who distances himself from the Mysteries distances himself from God. But he who receives Communion frequently, takes in the Savior frequently. For that saving voice says: "He that eateth My flesh, and drinketh My blood, dwelleth in Me, and I in him" (Jn. 6:56). This, then, is profitable for monks: for them to continuously remember the saving passion, and for them to be ready every day through preparing themselves and making themselves worthy at all times to receive the Holy and heavenly Mysteries, for in this way we are deemed worthy also of the forgiveness of sins. (52, PG 34, 1148A–1148B).

Also look ahead to Objection 7 where St. Jerome reports an encounter with this same Abba Apollo.

commune more frequently in order to become perfect, as we have already said.

If an infant is unable to grow into a man without bodily food, how much more must the soul be unable to arrive at perfection without spiritual food? Those wise in the things of this world say that there are three things apparent in an infant: first, that which is nourished; second, that through which it is nourished; and third, that which nourishes. That which nourishes is the nourishing soul; that which is nourished is the living (ensouled) body; and that with which it is nourished is food.

This, says Gabriel of Philadelphia, is also seen in the spiritual rebirth: "There is the one nourished, namely, the baptized and reborn man; that by which he is nourished, which is the immaculate Mysteries; and that which is nourishing, that is, the divine grace which changes them into the body and blood of our Savior." For this reason, Basil the Great says: "He who has been reborn through Baptism must be nourished by partaking of the divine Mysteries.[167]

But if, again, these objectors receive Communion as sinners, they should commune neither every forty days nor even once a year, as John Chrysostom says:

> Just as he who has a pure conscience should commune every day, so the one who finds himself in sins and unrepentant should not commune even during a Feast. For if we commune unworthily, even if once a year, we are not liberated from our offenses. Rather, this condemns us all the more, because, even though we only commune once a year, we still, even then, do not commune as pure. For this reason I ask all of you not to receive the divine Mysteries haphazardly and just because it is a Feast.[168]

And elsewhere he says:

---

167 *De Baptismo* 1.3, PG 31, 1573A; *Saint Basil: Ascetical Works*, 386.
168 *De Beato Philogonio* 4, PG 48, 755. [Translator's note: St. John continues: "But whoever intends to partake of this Holy Offering, let him purify himself many days beforehand through repentance and prayer and almsgiving."]

For since the priests cannot know who are sinners, and who unworthily partake of the Holy Mysteries, God often... delivers such people to Satan. For when diseases, attacks, sorrows, calamities, and the like afflict them, it is on this account. This is shown by Paul, who says: "For this cause many are weak and sickly among you, and many sleep" (1 Cor. 11:30). "But how can this be," someone says, "when we approach but once a year?" This is what is terrible, that you determine the worthiness of your approach, not by the purity of your mind, but by intervals of time. You think it is pious not to commune frequently, not knowing that you are seared by partaking unworthily even if just one time. But to receive worthily, even if frequently, is salvific. It is not bold to commune frequently, but to receive unworthily, even if one receives unworthily but once in his whole life. But we are so miserably foolish, that, though we commit thousands of evils in the course of a year, we are not anxious to be absolved of them, but are satisfied that we do not boldly and frequently dare to insult the body of Christ, not remembering that those who crucified Christ, crucified Him but once. Is the sin then the less, because committed but once? And Judas betrayed his Master but once. What then, did that exempt him from punishment? Why indeed is time to be considered in this matter? Let our hour of approaching the Mysteries be when our conscience is pure.[169]

Again the divine Chrysostom says:

What then? Whom shall we approve, those who receive Communion once a year? Those who receive many times? Those who receive a few times? Neither those who receive once, nor those who receive often, nor those who receive seldom, but those who come with a pure conscience, with a pure heart, and with an irreproachable life. Let such always draw near, but those who are not such, let them not approach

---

169 *On 1 Timothy* 5.3, PG 62, 529; NPNF [V1-13], 425.

even once. "Why?", you will ask. Because they thus receive to themselves judgment, condemnation, punishment, and vengeance.[170]

However (and I do not know why), those blessed people do not heed these things, and seek from those who would commune an angelic life and state. Now, that everyone who has been baptized and reborn through Holy Baptism has promised to live an angelic life is obvious. For the Christian, just as he is commanded to do, pushes himself to fulfill the Master's commandments as much as possible, and this is what is proper to the angelic orders: to always fulfill and perfect the divine commands.

So, then, in this way, those who have been baptized and keep the divine commandments are not far from the manner of life [*politeia*] of the angels, inasmuch as they take care to preserve in their body the purity of the bodiless powers, as the Apostle cries out: "Our citizenship [*politeuma*] is in heaven" (Phil. 3:20). And the divine Chrysostom says: "Let us then draw to us the invincible aid of the Spirit, keeping the commandments, and we will by no means be inferior to the angels."[171] And again he says: "The baptized and saved Christian receives a double grace. First, in that he is given life by the grace of the Holy Spirit; and, second, in that he becomes like a light bird, and flies freely to the heavens, living with the angels."[172]

OBJECTION 6

Some apply to divine Communion this saying from Proverbs: "If thou hast found honey, eat so much as is sufficient for thee, lest thou be filled therewith, and vomit it" (Pr. 25:16).

To these sophistries we are ashamed even to reply. For when we speak about honey as food, it is not with reference to the divine

---

170 *On Hebrews* 17.4, PG 63, 131–132; NPNF [V1-14], 449.

171 *On John* 75.5, PG 59, 409; NPNF (V1-14), 276.

172 Translator's note: This quote is actually from Bishop Severianos of Gabala (*De Mundi Creatione* 4.2, PG 56, 459). See footnote 148 above.

Mysteries, but to the delights proceeding from noetic spiritual vision and perfection, according to Gregory of Sinai and other Fathers. But if they take "honey" to mean the divine Gifts, then I hear the same writer of the Proverbs saying to me: "My son, eat thou honey, because it is good; and the honeycomb, which is sweet to thy taste. Thus shalt thou perceive wisdom in thy soul. For if thou find it, thine end shall be good, and hope shall not fail thee" (Pr. 24:13–14).[173]

In any case, they must explain to us what they understand by "sufficient," for we have no other way to measure the frequency of Communion except by the sacred Canons of the Apostles, and the whole Church of Christ. That is, to commune either four times a week (and if possible even every day), as Basil[174] and the divine Chrysostom[175] discuss, or at least every Saturday and Sunday and the other Feast Days, as when the Apostle commands married couples to abstain from one another on these days so that they may commune in the divine Mysteries, saying: "Defraud ye not one the other, except it be with consent for a time, that ye may give yourselves to fasting and prayer" (1 Cor. 7:5).[176]

---

173 Translator's note: And St. Nikodemos interprets Proverbs 9:1–5 as a call to frequent Communion and as a clear prophecy of the Christian Sacrifice: "Wisdom hath builded her house, she hath hewn out her seven pillars. She hath slaughtered her sacrifices; she hath mingled her wine; she hath also furnished her table. She hath sent forth her servants, calling with a loud proclamation to the feast, saying…. Come, eat of my bread, and drink of the wine which I have mingled" (Pr. 9:1–5) (See *Heortodromion*, vol. 2, 130–137, and *Pedalion*, 5–6; *The Rudder*, 6).

174 Cf. *Epistola* 93, PG 32, 484B; NPNF (V2-08), 179.

175 Cf. *Adversus Judaeos* 3.4, PG 48, 867.

176 Translator's note: Interpreting this passage of St. Paul, St. Nikodemos writes:

The married couple is to especially abstain from marital relations when they intend to receive the divine Mysteries. Then, they must abstain for at least three days prior to receiving Communion. I say this concerning the times outside of the fast periods when they happen to commune, because during the days of fasting when they commune, they also [in addition to food] abstain from relations on account of the fast. (*Hermeneia eis tas 14 Epistolas tou Apostolou Paulou* [*Explanation of the Fourteen Epistles of the Apostle Paul*], vol. 1 [Thessaloniki: Orthodoxos Kypsele, 1989], 461).

Also see St. Nikodemos' commentary on Canon 13 of the Sixth Ecumenical Council (*Pedalion*, 230; *The Rudder*, 306-307). And St. Symeon of Thessaloniki writes:

The fourteenth and fifteenth question ask similar things: whether an ordained man

As Timothy of Alexandria states: "They are to abstain from coming together on Saturday and Sunday, on account of the spiritual sacrifice which is offered to God on those days."[177] That is, on these days the Divine Liturgy is celebrated so that they may receive Communion.

And, concerning Feasts, the divine Gregory Palamas of Thessaloniki says:

> One day of the week… is called the Lord's day (Sunday), because it is consecrated to the Lord, Who on that day arose from the dead, disclosing and giving prior assurance of the general resurrection, when every earthly activity will come to an end. And you must not engage in any worldly activity that is not essential; and you must allow those who are under your authority and those who live with you to rest, so that

---

should know his wife the day he celebrates the Liturgy, and if he should know her after celebrating the Liturgy. Such things, my brother, are works of negligence and of bad judgment, for Paul says: "He who is engaged in ascetic struggle exercises self-control in all things" (1 Cor. 9:25). If they who were deemed worthy to see Mt. Sinai smoking and to hear the sound of the trumpet were given a command not to come near a women for three days (cf. Ex. 19:15), and if the priest Ahimelech asked David if he had been with a woman the previous night when David asked to eat the bread of the Presence, and only when David confessed that he had not [been with a woman for three days] did Ahimelech dare give him that bread to eat, which was a type [of the Heavenly Bread] (cf. 1 Kg. [1 Sam.] 21:1–6), who, then, would dare be so bold as to approach the Altar after coming together with his wife? Especially if even on the night before the Sacrifice when, if one happens to have a nocturnal fantasy, one must be reverent and draw back, as we have been taught?… Therefore, let those who are in sacred orders keep themselves pure prior to liturgizing, and also the day of the Liturgy, for they are sanctified by Communion, and God must not have communion with the flesh…. If someone must exercise self-control in order to see the glory of God and in order to pray, how much more necessary is it, then, that one exercise self-control when he intends on liturgizing and partaking of the most-dread Mysteries? (*Responsa ad Gabrielem Pentapolitanum*, Questions 14 and 15, PG 155, 864D–868A).

177 Canon 13 (*Pedalion*, 672; *The Rudder*, 897). [Translator's note: St. Nikodemos actually references here, by mistake, Canon 4 of Dionysios of Alexandria. Note, however, that Canon 3 of Dionysios of Alexandria (*Pedalion*, 549; *The Rudder*, 720) addresses the same subject, as does Canon 5 of Timothy of Alexandria (*Pedalion*, 668; *The Rudder*, 892).]

together you may all glorify Him Who redeemed us through His death and Who arose from the dead and resurrected our human nature with Himself. You should bring to mind the age to come and meditate upon all the commandments and statutes of the Lord, and you should examine yourself to see whether you have transgressed or overlooked any of them, and you should correct yourself in all ways. On this day you should go to the temple of God and attend the services held there, and with sincere faith and a clean conscience you should receive the holy body and blood of Christ. You should make a beginning of a more perfect life and renew and prepare yourself for the reception of the eternal blessings to come.... In this way you will sanctify the sabbath, observing it by doing no evil deeds. To the Lord's day you should join the days dedicated to the great feasts, doing the same things and abstaining from the same things.[178]

OBJECTION 7

Some, on account of their fearlessness toward God, call frequent Communion a heresy. They say that, just as those who are baptized outside of the tradition of the Church are heretics, likewise are those people who commune frequently heretics.

We are bewildered by such audacious words and, in truth, do not know what to say. We say only this: that, according to such an opinion, it follows that all of the Saints are heretics, and not only those who encouraged the faithful to receive divine Communion, but also those who accepted their words. And so are all of the priests who daily celebrate and partake of Communion (what blasphemy they say!), and indeed St. Apollo, who was greatly renowned for

---

178 *A New Testament Decalogue* 4, *GrPhilokalia*, 951–952; trans. *The Philokalia*, vol. 4, 326.

his holiness and had five thousand disciples in his care. The divine Jerome, who sought him out, writes concerning him:

> After we had prayed, washed our feet, and stood at table, they treated us spiritually and bodily, that is, we partook of the divine Mysteries with them, as they do every day.
>
> Then, after the meal, while we rested, they went out into the desert to pray on their knees until the morrow, until the time for service came. And after the ninth hour and vespers, they communed. After Communion, some sat and ate, while the more fervent went to practice stillness, living only by the strength of divine Communion. He of blessed memory told us many things profitable to the soul, primarily that we should commune in the divine Mysteries daily, and that we should receive strangers as if they were angels of God, as did Abraham, Lot, and others, for "upon these two commandments hang the whole Law and the Prophets" (Mt. 22:40).

Since, then, all the members of the choir of the divine Fathers are confessed as Saints and genuine servants of Christ, it follows that those who speak in opposition to them are also opposed to the Apostles, the Ecumenical and Local Holy Councils, and the Saints. And they are not only opposed to these, but also to the Lord Himself, Who says: "Whoso eateth My flesh, and drinketh My blood, hath eternal life" (Jn. 6:54). And again: "This do in remembrance of Me" (Lk. 22:19), that is, every day and always, according to the interpretation of the divine Chrysostom, as we said previously.

St. Timothy of Alexandria even allows demoniacs to receive Communion every Sunday, if they do not blaspheme the divine Gifts: "If one of the faithful is possessed by a demon, but does not deny the Mystery or blaspheme it in any way, let him receive Communion. Not, however, every day, for it is sufficient for him to receive only on Sunday."[179]

---

179 Canon 3 (*Pedalion*, 667; *The Rudder*, 891).

So, the divine Fathers allow not only those who are healthy, but also those who are demoniacs, to partake frequently of the divine Mysteries, while those blessed people who object to what we have said do not even allow those who are of a sound mind to commune, but rather seek to appear more lawful than the law.

OBJECTION 8

Some object saying: "Being human beings, are Christians not disturbed by gluttony, vainglory, laughter, idle talk, and other like passions? How, then, can they frequently commune?"

St. Anastasios of Antioch responds to these people saying:

> There are many people who, on account of their infrequent Communion, fall into sins. There are others who commune more frequently, and therefore greatly protect themselves from many evils, fearing the judgment of Holy Communion. Therefore, if we fall into some small, pardonable sins on account of our being human, either with our tongue, or our ears, or our eyes, and we fall as victims of deceit into vainglory, or sorrow, or anger, or some other like sin, let us condemn ourselves and confess to God. Thus let us partake of the Holy Mysteries, believing that the reception of the divine Mysteries is unto the remission of sins and purification. But if we also commit grave sins which are evil, carnal and impure, and we have rancor towards our brother, until we worthily repent of these sins, let us not boldly approach the divine Mysteries.
>
> But because we are human beings, bearing flesh and weaknesses, and pollute ourselves with many sins, God has given us various sacrifices unto the remission of our sins. If we offer these sacrifices to Him, they purify us in order that we may approach the Mysteries. Merciful almsgiving is a sacrifice which cleanses man from sins. There is also another

sacrifice which is unto salvation and the remission of sins, concerning which the Prophet David says, "A sacrifice unto God is a broken spirit; a heart that is broken and humbled God will not despise" (Ps. 50:17).

If we offer these sacrifices to God, and if we have some faults on account of being human, we will be able to approach Holy Communion with fear, trembling, and compunction, just as the woman with the issue of blood drew near to Christ, weeping and trembling.[180] There is sin which is unto death, there is sin which calls for the repentance we have described, and there is sin which requires bandaging [with a penance]. However, true repentance is able to heal all things. The person who approaches to partake of the Mysteries with fear, trembling, confession, and compunction receives forgiveness, while the person who communes without fear and with disdain receives punishment. Those who receive Communion disdainfully and unworthily not only do not receive forgiveness for their sins, but also are leapt at even more by the devil. But when Christians receive Communion with fear, not only are they sanctified, and do they receive forgiveness for their sins, but also is the devil driven far away from them.[181]

---

180 Cf. Mk. 5:25–34; Lk. 8:43–48.

181 Cf. *Quaestiones* 7, PG 89, 385C-389D. [Translator's note: Commenting on the words of the Divine Liturgy: "The Holy Things for the holy," St. Nicholas Cabasilas also says:

Those whom the priest calls holy are not only those who have attained perfection, but those also who are striving for it without having yet obtained it. Nothing prevents them from being sanctified by partaking of the Holy Mysteries, and from this point of view being saints…. The faithful are called saints because of the Holy Thing of which they partake, because of Him Whose body and blood they receive. Members of His body, flesh of His flesh and bone of His bone, as long as we remain united to Him and preserve our connection with Him, we live by holiness, drawing to ourselves, through the Holy Mysteries, the sanctity which comes from that Head and that Heart. But if we should cut ourselves off, if we should separate ourselves from the unity of this most holy body, we partake of the Holy Mysteries in vain, for life cannot flow into dead and amputated limbs. And what can cut off the members from this holy body? "It is

Even with all of these indisputable testimonies of the holy teachers of the Church, some still do not cease to dissent, but continue to raise objections.

OBJECTION 9

"At that time, the majority of Christians received Communion, while the minority did not. It is for this reason that the divine Fathers placed the minority under the rule of a Canon, so that the majority might not be scandalized. Today, however, since the majority of Christians do not receive Communion, barring a few, neither should these few commune, so that there may not be disorder in the Church and so that the majority may not be scandalized."

The people who say these things should, before contending that they are so, first know what exactly scandal and disorder mean. Scandal is that which distances a man from God and brings him near to the devil, according to Basil the Great: "Committing sin alienates us from the Lord and associates us with the devil."[182] And again he says: "Everything opposed to the will of the Lord is a scandal."[183] To say it more clearly, a scandal is any stumbling block placed in the road in order to trip up the person walking on it. The Prophet asks God to deliver him from these: "Keep me, O Lord, from the hand of the sinner; rescue me from unjust men who have

---

your sins which have separated Me from you" (Is. 59:2), says God. Does all sin then bring death to man? No indeed, but mortal sin only; that is why it is called mortal. For according to St. John there are sins which are not mortal (cf. 1 Jn. 5:16-17). That is why Christians, if they have not committed such sins as would cut them off from Christ and bring death, are in no way prevented, when partaking of the Holy Mysteries, from receiving sanctification, not in name alone, but in fact, since they continue to be living members united to the Head. (*Sacrae Liturgiae Interpretatio* 36, PG 150, 448D-449B; trans. *A Commentary on the Divine Liturgy*, 88-89)].

182 *Moralia* 22.1, PG 31, 741B; *Saint Basil: Ascetical Works*, 103.

183 Ibid., 33.2, PG 31, 752A; *Saint Basil: Ascetical Works*, 111.

devised to undermine my steps. The proud (or the demons) have hid a snare for me, and with cords have they spread a snare for my feet; stumbling blocks (scandals) near the paths have they set for me" (Ps. 139:4–5).

Seeing as the minority in this same way scandalized the majority at that time, drawing them into negligence and transgression of the commandment of God, and now the majority scandalizes the minority, thus pulling them into violation of the commandment, what should be done? Just as at that time the minority cut off their own wills and followed the majority in doing the will of God, so now the majority must cut off their wills and follow the minority in doing the will of God. The opposite should not happen; namely, the minority should not forsake the command of God just because they are few, and follow the majority into transgression of the commandment. For if this is how matters ought to proceed, the Prophet Elias, the Apostles, and so many other Fathers—as many, that is, as struggled on behalf of the truth—should have hid the truth and followed the majority, for they were in the minority. For this reason Basil the Great says: "Regarding the things which are according to the will of the Lord, even though some may be scandalized, one must demonstrate courageous boldness."[184]

But if some say that they are unable to see others communing frequently without being scandalized, let them understand for themselves that this is the result of either envy or hatred of their brother.

So, we cannot disdain the commandments of God in order that men not be scandalized, as Chrysostom says:

> Only up to this point should we think about not scandalizing men: that we do not give and afford them a handle against us. But if, though we give no such opportunity to them, they choose to criticize us thoughtlessly and without discrimination, let us laugh and weep because of their foolishness. Try to do "good things in the sight of the Lord and in the sight of men" (2 Cor. 8:21). If, though you do

---

184 Ibid., 33.5, PG 31, 753B; *Saint Basil: Ascetical Works*, 113.

good things, he still derides, have no more concern over it…. And Christ spoke thus about those who are scandalized: "Let them alone: they be blind leaders of the blind" (Mt. 15:14)…. For if the scandal is caused by us, then woe unto us; but, if it is not caused by us, it is not so. And again: Woe unto you through whom "the name of God is blasphemed" (Rom. 2:24). What then? If I do something that is good, but another blasphemes, that is nothing to me, but (a sin) only to him. For through him was God blasphemed…. When that which is pleasing to God is hindered by another's being scandalized, we should be concerned about this: that we not be forced because of him to offend God.

Tell me, if, while we are discoursing and putting drunkards to shame, someone is scandalized, should I stop speaking?… It is always good to know the right mean. Many reviled because a certain beautiful virgin remained as she was (and did not marry, but became a nun), and they criticized those who catechized her (the priests who made her a nun). What then? Was it their duty to desist for that (and not tonsure her a nun)? By no means. For, on the contrary, they were doing nothing wrong, but rather, a very virtuous deed pleasing to God…. On all occasions it behooves us to follow the laws of God, to take great pains that we give no occasion for scandal, so that we may be innocent and be deemed worthy of enjoying God's philanthropy.[185]

So much concerning scandal. Concerning disorder, this is when something occurs out of order. Since, as we said earlier, it is the order and law of the Church for those Christians who are present at the Divine Liturgy to receive Communion (that is, as many as are not prohibited because they are under a rule), it follows then that as many as do not receive Communion are clearly causing disorder, transgressing the laws of the Church. On this account the Prophet Habakkuk says: "The sun was exalted, and the moon stood

---

185 *On Acts* 46.3, PG 60, 324–325; NPNF (V1-11), 281-282.

still in her course (order)" (Hab. 3:11). That is to say, the Sun of Righteousness,[186] Christ our God, was raised onto the Cross; and the moon, that is, the Church, stayed in her course and in order; which means that the Church held fast to the will and command of God, from which she had fallen.[187] Therefore, those who do what is outside of the commandment of God are the ones who cause scandals and disorder, and not those who struggle as much as they can to keep the Master's commandments.

OBJECTION 10

Still others bring up the *Tome of Union* and say that there is a Canon written in the Horologion[188] which designates that Christians should receive Communion three times a year.

Regarding this Canon these blessed people bring forth, even though it is a fabrication and false addition—or even if it be correct—I ask them, please, to tell me: is it just and right that this Canon should have more authority than the so great a number of trumpets of the Holy Spirit that have been cited thus far? The imperial laws write that any law written by an emperor that is found to be contrary to the sacred Canons and divine Fathers is rendered void. The divine Chrysostom says that a custom or habit contrary to the divine laws is to be terminated. Again he says: "Habit is a difficult thing, and it is hard to break and hard to avoid.... Therefore, the more you understand the power of a habit, the more should you endeavor to be rid of a bad habit and change yourself over to a good one."[189]

---

186 Mal. 4:2.

187 Translator's note: For a more detailed commentary on this passage of the Fourth Ode (Hab. 3:2–19), see St. Nikodemos' work, *Kepos Chariton* [*Garden of Graces*], which interprets the Nine Odes ([Thessaloniki: Regopoulos, 1992], 112–114).

188 Translator's note: The *Horologion* or *Book of the Hours* is the service book of the Orthodox Church used in the daily cycle of services.

189 *Ad Illuminandos Catecheses* 1.5, PG 49, 230; *St. John Chrysostom: Baptismal Instructions* (New York: Paulist Press, ACW, 1963), 145.

How, then, do they seek to support their soul-destroying habit? Since they seek to hide the truth with this Canon, we will briefly show its true meaning, so that the truth may be clearly revealed and no one deceived any longer.

The Canon came about for the following reason: Leo the Wise, because he married for a fourth time, was excommunicated by the then-Patriarch Nicholas. The emperor deposed Nicholas from the throne because the patriarch did not want to allow him a fourth marriage, and put on the throne in his stead Euthymios, who then loosed the Emperor from his excommunication. Owing to these events, the hierarchs and the people were divided into two factions, some siding with Patriarch Nicholas, and others with Euthymios.

After Emperor Leo died, his brother Alexander reigned in his stead, and he deposed Euthymios from the patriarchal throne and restored it to Nicholas. When Alexander too died, his nephew, Constantine Porphyrogennetos, the son of Leo the Wise, reigned. His father-in-law, Romanos, had the title of *Basilopator* (father of the emperor). Constantine and Romanos convened a Council in the year 922 A.D. This Council not only prohibited fourth marriages, but also drew up the following Canon against third marriages, which says:

> Regarding anyone who is forty years old, and is not ashamed of his age or does not heed the modest life required of Christians, but is provoked to marry for a third time only because of the desires of the flesh, we decree that he is not to partake of Holy Communion for five years. This is to be observed in all strictness, and no one has permission to lessen the years of excommunication. After the five years have passed and he is deemed worthy to commune, he is not allowed to approach Communion at any other time except during the saving Resurrection of Christ our God, purifying himself beforehand as much as possible by the fast of Holy Lent. But whoever is thirty years old and has children from his previous marriage, and then wishes to take a third wife, is not allowed to partake of Holy Communion for four years. After the four years pass and he is permitted to

partake of the Mysteries, he is allowed to receive only three times a year: during the Feasts of the saving Resurrection of Christ our God, the Dormition of our immaculate Lady the Theotokos, and the Birth of Christ, for there is a fast preceding each of these Feasts, and from fasting one receives benefit and cleansing.[190]

This Act of the Council was named the *Tome of Union* because it united the hierarchs and the rest of the people who had been divided on account of the fourth marriage of Leo.

I do not know what blessed person, either on account of illiteracy or out of desire to block Christians from eternal life, maimed this Canon and placed it in its mutilated condition into the *Horologion*. And then, our blessed Spiritual Fathers, finding it, spread it throughout the world, placing the penance of a third marriage upon all Christians, whether married for a second time, or just once, or virgin, and upon those of all ages.

I am not amazed so much by the Spiritual Fathers, but by the good hierarchs and shepherds who did not immediately sound the horn with the God-inspired trumpets of truth, in order to castigate the evil sower of that weed and uproot from the Church that dead plant. For they have the authority by the grace of the Holy Spirit to sustain that which is good and to correct whatever is in need of correction.

Perhaps the hierarchs make the excuse that, since they are under the yoke of the Ottomans and caught up in many concerns, they entrust these things to the teachers and preachers. These blessed hierarchs, one not wanting to lose his quietude, and another making other excuses—all of them together abdicate their responsibility and throw the burden one upon the other. So they bury the word of God and the truth as if in a tomb. And by their silence they show that they acquiesce to all the things which are happening, as the divine Meletios the Confessor says:

---

190 In the Acts of the Council, vol. 2, 975.

"He who possesses knowledge of the truth,
And, in whatever way, deliberately hides it,
Not openly preaching it or speaking it with boldness,
And does not uphold the divine and august Canons,
Or the laws presided over by the Fathers,
Is justly punished no less than the transgressors of these.
He who is silent about the truth hides Christ in a tomb,
As one Father has said, and another, again, says.
He who is silent about the faith is in grave danger
Of eternal punishment and of the pit of perdition.
It is not just, lawful, or right for the faithful to be silent
When the laws of God are being violated,
And the evil seek to support their deception.
When someone is in danger of being separated from God,
Said one of the great Fathers,
And when evils are attributed to God,
What faithful Christian can be silent? Who can be at peace?
For silence means consent and betrayal,
As was clearly shown by the Lord's Forerunner
And the brave Maccabees together with him,
Who, on account of the smallest commandment, were in danger unto death,
And did not even betray the smallest part of the Law.
War is many times known to be praiseworthy,
And battle appears better than soul-destroying peace.
For it is better to stand against those who do not believe correctly,
Than it is to follow them and be of one mind with them,
Thus being united with them and separated from God."[191]

And the divine Chrysostom says, "If it is not good for a man to be silent when he is wronged, how will one who remains silent and indifferent when the divine laws are insulted not be worthy of punishment?"[192]

---

191 *Alphabetalphabetos*, Hypothesis 10 (Thessaloniki: 1923).

192 *De Sancta Babyla, Contra Julianum et Gentiles* 9, PG 50, 547.

OBJECTION 11

Many object and say that for someone to receive Communion is not a dogma of the faith, which must be kept obligatorily.

Even if frequent Communion is not a dogma of the faith, it is nevertheless found to be a commandment of the Master included in His other sayings, especially when He says: "This do in remembrance of Me" (Lk. 22:19). That is, "Do this frequently and every day, as long as the present age lasts." And for this reason, being that it is a commandment of the Master, it must necessarily be kept as we said previously, in the first part of this book.

As many as raise this objection show by this that they want to strip the dogmas, leaving them bereft of every ecclesiastical formulation and legislation. We, however, ask them, how then can dogmas be supported? Did not the divine Chrysostom previously tell us that our Christian manner of life requires correct dogmas, and that dogmas require a pure life? And that a pure manner of life is born of and attained through the divine commandments, the sacred laws of the Church, and the venerable traditions and formulations of the divine Fathers? If, then, we violate the divine Canons, the Master's commandments, and the rest, our pure manner of life will be destroyed. When a pure manner of life is destroyed, we also lose correct dogmas, and will be left barren and without light.

There is not sufficient time to enumerate the thousands of Saints who suffered and died for the ecclesiastical laws and Canons. There are, on the other hand, some who are so audacious that they not only do not suffer for the truth, but also actually oppose the truth. And they boldly refute the Master's commands by prohibiting from divine Communion those who approach, for no reason at all and without them having committed any offense. This is something very bold, for not even did our Lord turn away Judas from Communion, though He knew that he was an abominable vessel of wickedness. Christ daily receives all who would partake of Communion. The worthy He purifies, illumines, and sanctifies. The unworthy He first turns over to their convicting conscience, and then, if they

amend their ways, receives them with compassion. If they remain
uncorrected, He gives them over to various illnesses, as the Apostle
says, for since many in his time were receiving Communion
unworthily, they were becoming ill on this account, and many were
dying.[193]

Those blessed people who raise this objection prohibit the
Orthodox from divine Communion without even knowing the
spiritual condition of the communicants, and only to sustain their
bad habit and evil custom, which has prevailed unto the detriment
of their souls.

But let us ask Basil the Great to speak to us the truth:

> Question 11: Whether it is right or safe to refuse to obey any
> of the commands of God, or to impede the one who has
> been commanded to do them, or to be tolerant of those who
> are doing the impeding, especially if the person impeding is
> genuine and close to God, or if some seemingly plausible
> reason impede the accomplishment of the command.
>
> Reply: Considering the Lord's words: "Learn of Me, for I
> am meek and lowly in heart" (Mt. 11:29), it is clear that we
> are more solidly instructed in all things when we recall the
> words of our Lord Jesus Christ Himself, the Only-begotten
> Son of the living God. Therefore: When John the Baptist
> said to Him, "I have need to be baptized of Thee, and
> comest Thou to me?" (Mt. 3:14), He replied, "Suffer it to be
> so now, for so it becometh us to fulfill all righteousness" (Mt.
> 3:15). Again, in the presence of the disciples, when Peter
> decried the sufferings which the Lord prophesied He must
> undergo in Jerusalem, He said with great displeasure, "Get
> thee behind Me, Satan, thou art a scandal unto Me; for thou
> savourest not the things that be of God, but those that be of
> men" (Mt. 16:23). On another occasion, when Peter, moved
> by reverence toward his Master, refused His ministration,

---

193 Cf. 1 Cor. 11:30.

the Lord again said, "If I wash thee not, thou hast no part with Me" (Jn. 13:8).

And if the soul requires further assistance from examples taken from persons like ourselves, let us recall the words of the Apostle: "What mean ye to weep and to break mine heart? For I am ready not to be bound only, but also to die at Jerusalem for the Name of the Lord Jesus" (Acts 21:13). Who could be more admirable than John? Or more sincere than Peter? Or what motives could have been more reverential than those which they alleged? I know, furthermore, that neither Moses, that holy man, nor the Prophet Jonah remained blameless before God when they entertained thoughts that were contrary to obedience. By these examples we are taught neither to contradict, nor to impede, nor to tolerate those who impede others.

And if the word of the Scripture teaches beyond a doubt that we dare not perform these particular actions or others like them, how much greater is our obligation to imitate the Saints with regard to the rest when they say, "We ought to obey God rather than men" (Acts 5:29) and, "Whether it be right in the sight of God to hearken unto you more than unto God, judge ye. For we cannot but speak the things which we have seen and heard" (Acts 4:19–20).[194]

And again Basil says,

No one must impede the person who is doing the will of God, whether he does it because of a commandment of God, or for some other reason related to a commandment; nor ought the doer of the will of God to permit any to hinder him, even though they be genuine friends of God, but he should remain steadfast in his decision.... The person who does a commandment of God without sincerity, and yet maintains in appearance the exactness of the Lord's

---

194 *De Baptismo* 2, Question 11, PG 31, 1621B–1624A; *Saint Basil: Ascetical Works*, 425-426.

teaching, should not be impeded, because no one is harmed insofar as the act itself is concerned, and sometimes certain people may be benefited by it; yet such a person should be exhorted to have a disposition worthy of his good action.[195]

And: "We should not follow human traditions to the extent of violating the commandment of God.... No one may prefer his own will to the will of the Lord, but in everything we must seek and do the will of God."[196]

The divine Chrysostom says:

> We must bravely stand against whatever prevents us from that good desire. Listen to what Christ says: "He that loveth father or mother more than Me is not worthy of Me" (Mt. 10:37). For whenever we do something that is according to the will of God, we must consider whatever prevents us as our enemy and opponent, whether father, or mother, or anyone else.[197]

Ignatios the Godbearer says: "Every one that teaches anything besides what is commanded, even if he is credible, even if he fasts, even if he lives celibately, even if he works miracles, even if he prophesies, let him be in your sight as a wolf in sheep's clothing, laboring for the destruction of the sheep."[198]

And the divine Meletios the Confessor says:
> *"Do not listen to monks or to presbyters,*
> *When they wrongly counsel you and lead you astray.*
> *What—only monks? And only presbyters?*
> *Do not even listen to bishops when they advise you*
> *To do and to say and to believe that which harms the soul."*

---

195 *Moralia* 19.1 and 2 PG 31, 733A and 736A; *Saint Basil: Ascetical Works*, 97, 99.

196 Ibid., 12.2 and 4, PG 31, 724A and 724D; *Saint Basil: Ascetical Works*, 89, 90.

197 *De Virginitate* 78.5, SC 125, 374.

198 *To Heron the Deacon of Antioch* 2, PG 5, 912A–912B; ANF (01), 113.

OBJECTION 12

Some are scandalized because what they say, especially concerning the prohibition from frequent Communion, does not convince us, and they hold up the following things in their defense: First, that the Canons and commandments are under the authority of the hierarchs. Second, that we are not to examine what hierarchs, teachers, and Spiritual Fathers tell us, but only to obey simply everything they say. And third, they put forth the Apostolic saying: "Obey them that have the rule over you, and submit yourselves" (Heb. 13:17).

To this three-part objection we personally have nothing to say, so that we may not cause some of the people to be upset and disturbed. To say nothing to these things, however, we think would be harmful to the soul. Wherefore, let us see what the Saints say, so that no one can complain.

Basil the Great responds to the first part of the objection saying:

> For if the Lord Himself, in Whom the Father was well pleased, "in Whom are hid all the treasures of wisdom and knowledge" (Col. 2:3), Who having received all authority and all judgment from the Father says, "He gave Me a commandment, what I should say, and what I should speak" (Jn. 12:49); and again, "Whatsoever I speak therefore, even as the Father said unto Me, so I speak" (Jn. 12:50); and the Holy Spirit speaks not from Himself, but whatever things He hears from Him, those He speaks[199]—how much more is it both pious and safe for us to think and do this (that is, not to transgress the divine commandments, but to be willingly obedient to them)?[200]

---

199 Cf. Jn. 16:13.
200 *De Fide* PG 31, 677A–677B; *Saint Basil: Ascetical Works*, 57-58.

The divine Chrysostom shows from the very ordination of hierarchs that the hierarchs are subject to the divine Canons and commandments, saying:

> Since the high priest (of the Old Law) was the head of the people, he himself (being the head) was also to be under an authority, for an authority not subject to a higher authority is unbearable; so, by his having the sign of authority over his head, it was indicated that he was under a law. It is ordered (by the Law) that the head be not bare, but covered, in order to teach the head of the people that he too has a head (an authority) over him. This is why during the ordination of a priest in the Church the Gospel of Christ is placed upon his head, so that he may learn that he is receiving the true tiara (authority) of the Gospel. (Here the word "priest" takes the place of "hierarch," being used according to the general sense of the priesthood, for, to quote Dionysios the Areopagite, only hierarchs wear "the words handed down by God" upon their heads.)[201] It is also so that he may learn that, even though he is head of all, he is nevertheless under the laws (of the Gospel); and that, while he has authority over all the other laws, he himself is under the authority of the laws; and also that, while he enacts all other laws, he himself is governed by the law. For this reason, one of the brave ancients (the Hieromartyr Ignatios), who was illustrious in the priesthood and in martyrdom, wrote to a certain priest (that is, a hierarch, Polycarp) saying: "Let nothing be done without your consent; neither should you do anything without the approval of God."[202] So, the fact that the hierarch has the Gospel on his head is a sign that he is under its authority.[203]

---

201 Cf. *De Ecclesiastica Hierarchia* 5.2 and 5.3.1 and 7, PG 3, 509B, 509C and 513C; *Pseudo-Dionysius: The Complete Works*, 239-240, 242.

202 *To Polycarp* 4, SC 10, 174; ANF (01), 94.

203 *De Legislatore* 4, PG 56, 464.

Regarding the second part of the objection, that we should not examine what hierarchs, teachers, and Spiritual Fathers tell us, but be obedient in all things, Basil the Great responds to it saying:

> He who is in charge of preaching the word (that is, whether he is a teacher or a hierarch) must do and say everything with great deliberation and judgment, aiming at pleasing God, inasmuch as he must be tested and borne witness to by the very people who are entrusted to him.[204]

Again he says: "The hearers that have been instructed in the Scriptures should test what their teachers say. Those things that are in agreement with the Scriptures they should accept, but should reject that which disagrees; and they should reject even more those who persist in such teachings."[205] Next he says: "Those who have little knowledge of the Scriptures should be able to recognize those who are holy and Saints by the fruits of the Spirit they exhibit. And they should receive the people who display these as Saints, but reject those that do not."[206] Elsewhere he writes: "One must not be easily carried away by those who feign the truth, without examining them, but one must investigate each man with the help of the test given by Scripture."[207] And once more: "Every word or thing should be confirmed by the testimony of the divinely inspired Scripture, so those who are good may be assured, and so that those who are bad may be ashamed."[208]

The divine Chrysostom responds to the third part of the objection, saying:

> Anarchy is an evil, and the occasion of many calamities, and the source of disorder and confusion…. But no less an evil also is the disobedience to rulers…. But perhaps someone will say that there is also a third evil, when the ruler is bad. I

---

204 *Morales* 70.37, PG 31, 844D–845A; *Saint Basil: Ascetical Works*, 184.
205 Ibid. 72.1, PG 31, 845D–848A; *Saint Basil: Ascetical Works*, 185-186.
206 Ibid. 72.2, PG 31, 848B; *Saint Basil: Ascetical Works*, 186.
207 Ibid. 28.1, PG 31, 748A; *Saint Basil: Ascetical Works*, 108.
208 Ibid. 26.1, PG 31, 744C; *Saint Basil: Ascetical Works*, 106.

myself also know this, and no small evil it is, but a far worse evil even than anarchy. For it is better to be led by no one than to be led by one who is evil. For the former indeed are oftentimes saved and oftentimes in peril, but the latter will be altogether in peril, being led into the pit of destruction. How then does Paul say: 'Obey them that have the rule over you, and submit yourselves' (Heb. 13:17)?

Having said above, "Whose faith follow, considering the end of their behavior" (Heb. 10:7), he then says, "Obey them that have the rule over you, and submit yourselves." "What then," you say, "when he is evil, should we obey?" Evil? In what sense? If indeed in regard to faith, flee and avoid him; not only if he is a man, but even if he is an angel come down from heaven. But if in regard to life, do not be over-curious…. For hear Christ saying: "The Scribes and the Pharisees sit on Moses' seat" (Mt. 23:2). Having previously spoken many fearful things concerning them, He then says: "They sit on Moses' seat: all therefore whatsoever they tell you observe, do; but do not ye after their works" (Mt. 23:2–3). They have, He means, the dignity of office, but are of unclean life. Attend, however, not to their life, but to their words.

For as regards their characters, no one would be harmed thereby. How is this? Both because their characters are manifest to all, and also because though he were ten thousand times as wicked, he will never teach what is wicked. But as respects faith, the evil is not manifest to all, and the wicked ruler will not shrink from teaching it. Moreover, "Judge not that ye be not judged" (Mt. 7:1) concerns life, [though] not faith.

Paul, however, has previously commended the shepherds (namely, has borne witness to the fact that they are sound in all things), and after this he says "Obey them that have the rule over you."[209]

And elsewhere St. John again says:

"But so and so," someone says, "is a good man and a priest and lives a life of temperance and piety." Do not speak to me of that good, temperate, pious priest! Let it be, if you wish, Peter or Paul or even an angel who has come down from heaven. Not even in such cases do I regard the dignity of persons. I do not recognize the law of any servant, but only the King's law. When we read what the King has written, let His servant, however high his office, be silent....

Why do you bring up the case of this man or that man? God will not acquit you because of the negligence of your fellow servants, but He will judge you according to the precept of His laws. "I commanded," He will say to you on the day of judgment, "you should have obeyed My command and not used this man and that man as an excuse, and concerned yourself with the evils of others." Tell me, is it safe for us to sin because the great David committed a grievous sin? This is all the more reason why we must be on our guard and emulate only the good works of the Saints. If we find negligence or transgression of the law anywhere, we must flee from it with great zeal. Our account is rendered not to our fellow servants but to the Master, and to him shall we give account for all we have done in our lives.[210]

So this is what the Saints say. But we, my brothers, since the Lord has called us in peace,[211] must obey the hierarchs, the Spiritual Fathers, and the teachers, on account of the dignity of the office which they have received from God. But if one of these is doing something irrational or prohibits us from doing some virtuous work,

---

209 *On Hebrews* 34.1, PG 63, 231–232; NPNF (V1-14), 518–519.
210 *Ad Illuminandos Catecheses* 1.5, PG 49, 229–230; *St. John Chrysostom: Baptismal Instructions*, 144.
211 Cf. Col. 3:15.

let us not cease from asking and beseeching him until we convince him and until the will of God is done, so that peace may reign among us; so that harmony and concord may prevail; so that there may be love between the Shepherds and the sheep, between the hierarchs and the Christian people, between the priests and the laity, and between the leaders and the led; and so that scandals, disturbances, schisms, and divisions be absent and far from us. For these things are what will destroy our souls, our homes, our churches, and every community and race. In brief, let us do all these things so that we may all be one body and one spirit, all with one hope, just as we were called,[212] so that the God of peace may also be with us.

OBJECTION 13

Some say: "Behold, we keep the commandment of the Lord and receive Communion two or three times a year, and this suffices as our apology."

To such people we reply that this too is good and beneficial. But for someone to recieve Communion more frequently is much better. The more one approaches light, the more he is illumined; the more he approaches fire, the more he is warmed; and the more he draws near to holiness, the more is he made holy. Wherefore, the more frequently someone approaches God through Communion, the more is he illumined, warmed, and made holy. My brother, if you are worthy to receive Communion two or three times a year, you are also worthy, just as the divine Chrysostom says, to receive more frequently, performing the same preparation. What prohibits us from communing? Our negligence and our sloth. Being conquered by these, we do not prepare ourselves according to our abilities.

We also reply in another way. Such people do not practice the commandment of God as they think. For where did God (or any of the Saints) command that we should receive Communion two or three times a year? This idea is not to be found anywhere. We must therefore know that, when we practice a commandment, we must

212 Cf. Eph. 4:4.

be careful to practice it according to the commandment. What I mean is that we must heed the place, time, purpose, manner, and all the circumstances under which we practice the commandment. This way the good will be perfect in everything and well-pleasing to God.[213]

The same applies to divine Communion. For someone to commune frequently is necessary, profitable to the soul, according to the commandment of God, perfectly good, and virtuous. But for someone to receive Communion only three times a year is neither according to a commandment nor perfectly good, for that which is not done in a good way is not good.

For this reason, just as the rest of the commandments of God demand to be performed at the time proper to each, according to the Ecclesiast: "There is a time for everything" (Ec. 3:17), so also does the commandment of divine Communion. We must afford the proper time to its performance, which is the moment when the priest cries out, "With the fear of God, with faith, and with love, draw near." Is this heard only three times a year? Alas and woe! And since the physical body needs to eat two or three times a day to live, does the poor soul then, in order to live the spiritual life, only need to eat its life-giving food three times a year, or even just once a year? Is not this a great absurdity? Otherwise, I fear—I fear that perhaps we do not profit from doing the commandments. For we adulterate them and corrupt them, and we are not doers of the law, but creators of anti-laws. While fasting on many occasions and

---

213 Translator's note: See St. Basil the Great's reply to the question, "Whether the work enjoined by the commandment is acceptable to God if the manner of performing it is not in conformity with the commandment of God" (*De Baptismo* 2, Question 8, PG 31, 1600A–1612A; *Saint Basil: Ascetical Works*, 407 ff). And St. Maximos the Confessor says: "In everything that we do God searches out our purpose to see whether we do it for Him or for some other motive" (*Second Century on Love* 36, *GrPhilokalia*, 304; *The Philokalia*, vol. 2, 71). Elsewhere, the divine Maximos says: "The demons do not hate self-restraint, fasting, almsgiving, hospitality, the singing of psalms… or any of the other things which characterize a life lived according to God, so long as the aim and purpose of a person trying to live such a life are tilted in their direction" (*Fifth Century on Various Texts of Theology* 70, *GrPhilokalia*, 402; *Third Century of Various Texts, The Philokalia*, vol. 2, 227–228).

thinking that we were fulfilling the commandment of God, we were actually sinning, as the divine Chrysostom says:

> Do not tell me that they are fasting; but show me that it is God's will that they fast. If it is not God's will, then their fasting is more unlawful than any drunkenness. For we must not only look at what they do, but also seek out the reason that they do it. What is done in accordance with God's will, even if it seems bad, is the best of all things. What is done contrary to God's will, even if it seems very good, is the worst and most unlawful of all things…. For it is God's will, and not the nature of things, that makes the same actions good or bad.[214]

EPILOGUE

Behold, my beloved brothers, that with the help of God the present book has come to an end, having clearly shown from the testimonies of the Holy Scripture and of the Saints that frequent communion of the immaculate Mysteries is necessary and most profitable to the soul, and that without this it is impossible for us to ascend to the love of our Lord, Who fashioned us from nonbeing, and again, after we had shattered, refashioned us.[215]

There is nothing else necessary now except to prepare ourselves properly through contrition, confession, and fulfilling our ascetical rule, and thus draw near to the Mysteries with fear and trembling to partake of them. Whoever of us desires life and longs to see good days, according to the Psalmist,[216] let him approach his Lord, the sweetest Jesus Christ, Who daily calls to us from the sacred Table saying, "Come, eat My bread and drink the wine which I have offered to you in the Holy Spirit, so that you may be illumined in both soul and body; so that you may be nourished and fed with the

214 *Adversus Judaeos* 4.1, PG 48, 873.

215 Cf. Ps. 2:9, and John Chrysostom, *Ad Illuminados Catacheses* 1.4, PG 49, 227; *St. John Chrysostom: Baptismal Instructions*, 139–140.

216 Cf. Ps. 33:12.

food of immortality, and be watered with the drink of incorruption and ambrosia, so that your faces shall not be ashamed in a time of need."[217]

While we still have time, "let us do good" (Gal. 6:10), according to the Apostle. "Behold, now is the accepted time; behold, now is the day of salvation" (2 Cor. 6:2). Let us pursue and follow the Lord, and, according to Hosea,[218] we will find Him ready like the dawn to enlighten us, and He will come to us, just as the early and late rain comes upon the earth. Let us hear Jeremiah, who says, "Stand ye in the ways, and see, and ask for the old paths, where is the good way, and walk therein" (Jer. 6:16). Let us repent with all of our soul and heart for our former negligence, and let us correct ourselves, so that we may not again hear the Prophet Jeremiah reprove and say:

> O Lord, are not Thine eyes upon the truth? Thou hast stricken them, but they have not grieved; Thou hast consumed them, but they have refused to receive correction: they have made their faces harder than a rock; they have refused to return…. The prophets prophesy falsely, and the priests bear rule by their means; and My people love to have it so…. To whom shall I speak, and give warning, that they may hear? Behold, their ear is uncircumcised, and they cannot hearken: behold, the word of the Lord is unto them a reproach; they have no delight in it…. For from the least of them even unto the greatest of them every one is given to covetousness; and from the prophet even unto the priest every one dealeth falsely." (Jer. 5:3, 31 and 6:10, 13).

Let us heed the words which profit our soul, not paying attention to who is saying them, whether he is a wise man or unwise, or well-known or humble. For what does it profit us if so-and-so is someone important and great? Or what does it harm us if so-and-so is humble and unimportant? We are not seeking to purchase the one or the other—only the words of Scripture are required for our benefit. And whether someone wise or someone unwise says them makes no

---

217 Cf. Ps. 33:5.
218 Cf. Hos. 6:3.

difference to us. For this reason we must compare what is said with what is written, and if they agree we will accept them. But if they disagree, we have need neither of the wise man's words nor of the unwise man's. For whoever goes to the market to buy wheat or some other thing does not pay attention to whether the person selling it is good or bad, but only pays attention to whether the product is good.

Wherefore, we must both heed the words with great care, and not transgress what the divine Fathers handed down to us, if we do not wish to stray from the straight path.

If the heretics had heeded the divine Scriptures, they would not have followed those first arch-heretics, to be destroyed together with them. The conniving devil sowed various heresies among them, and deprived them of, among other things, Holy Baptism. And he is again trying to destroy us Orthodox, by distancing us from frequently receiving divine Communion. Since he was not able to sway us from Holy Baptism, he is conniving to kill us through other means.

And do not think that the one differs from the other at all. Our Lord judged equally concerning them both, as we said previously. Because for someone not to be born at all, or for someone to die from starvation after he is born, do not differ in the least.

Thus we were reborn indeed by divine Baptism. If, however, we are not afterwards fed with frequent Communion in order to live the spiritual life, we will die of hunger for grace, and we will nearly fall into worse passions than the unbaptized.

For this reason, I beg of you, let us fear the words of our Lord now, while we are alive, just as we did when we found salvation, and so that we are not horrified at the future judgment, left without a single consolation. May we not resemble those to whom it was said: "Laying aside the commandment of God, ye hold the tradition of men" (Mk. 7:8).

Let us not be deceived by the superstitions and prejudices that have held sway, but let us heed what is written, as Basil the Great says: "A very evil custom deceives us, and a perverted human tradition is the source of great evils for us."[219] Again he says:

---

219 *De Judicio Dei*, PG 31, 669A.

If righteousness according to the Law that is sought by those who have consecrated themselves to God in Baptism and promised to "not henceforth live unto themselves, but unto Him which died for them, and rose again" (2 Cor. 5:15), is condemned as adultery...[220] what, then, should be said concerning the observances of human traditions?

...The denunciation of human traditions is clearly expressed by the words of the Lord,[221] but, as regards particular imaginations of human wisdom, the Apostle has instructed us to repudiate them with vigor. He says: "For the weapons of our warfare are not carnal, but mighty through God to the pulling down of strong holds, casting down imaginations, and every high thing that exalteth itself against the knowledge of God" (2 Cor. 10:4–5). Or with reference to individual conceptions of righteousness in general, even if it is earnestly sought after for God's sake.... From this and similar sayings it is clear that they who would quibble about the judgments of God are condemned. For it is written: "Woe unto them that are wise in their own eyes, and prudent in their own sight" (Is. 5:21).... It is necessary, therefore, to be pure from all alike—the lusts of the devil, worldly preoccupations, human traditions, and from our own desires, no matter how presentable they may seem.[222]

Let us not transgress the commandments of God and become on this account worse than the irrational beasts and more foolish than fish, which at least do not contradict the law of God. For as St. Basil again says: "Fish (which are dumb and irrational) do not contradict the (natural) law of God, while humans (who are 'rational') do not keep the saving teachings of God."[223]

Let us leave those who would live negligently. Rather, let us supplicate God to give them earnestness. Let us all awaken from the

---

220 Cf. Rom. 7:1–6.
221 Cf. Mt. 15:3ff.
222 *De Baptismo* 1.2.19, PG 31, 1557C–1560B; *Saint Basil: Ascetical Works*, 374-375, 376.
223 *In Hexaemeron* 7.4, SC 26bis, 412; NPNF (V2-08), 92.

slumber of sloth and receive fervor and love in our heart, so that we can obey the spiritual call of the priest, and let us approach the Mysteries with a broken and humbled heart.[224] It is great contempt towards God for such a multitude of Christians to attend the Divine Liturgy and then, when the Lord calls us through the priest to go and receive Communion, for not even one person out of such a multitude to be found to fulfill the divine call, and not because of any sin or other cause, but only on account of an evil custom and a bad habit.

Alas, my brothers! I fear that perhaps the Lord will also say concerning us: "None of those men which were bidden shall taste of My supper" (Lk. 14:24), and, furthermore, perhaps He will punish us even more severely, if we do not repent and correct ourselves.

I want to ask you this: If at the time of the Mystical Supper one of the Apostles said: "I do not want to receive Communion today," what would the Lord have said? Certainly, I believe, that just as He said to Peter at the sacred washing of the feet, "If I wash thee not, thou hast no part with Me" (Jn. 13:8), He would likewise have said to one not wanting to receive Communion at the divine Supper, "If thou dost not eat My body, and if thou dost not drink My blood, thou hast no part with Me."

Beloved, the Lord says this very same thing to us now at every Liturgy: "Except ye eat the flesh of the Son of Man... ye have no life in you" (Jn. 6:53). Patience is required of the one who is prohibited on account of his sins, because he has been placed under a rule by his Spiritual Father not to receive Communion. But to be deprived of such heavenly grace only on account of an evil custom? O wicked habit!

This most wicked custom has become so entrenched, that we not only do not receive Communion, but also, when we see others frequently receiving divine Communion, reproach them and judge them as if they were impious and scorners of the divine Mysteries, when actually we should be imitating them.

Rightly, then, has the prophecy of Isaiah been fulfilled in us: "And He said, Go, and tell this people, Hear ye indeed, but

---

224 Cf. Ps. 50:17.

understand not; and see ye indeed, but perceive not. Make the heart of this people fat, and make their ears heavy, and shut their eyes" (Is. 6:9–10). For, in truth, we have all become calloused and unfeeling, and we do not even understand what we are saying, nor anything we hear, nor anything we see.

And so deplorable is the condition in which we find ourselves, that I know that, no matter what I say or how much I say concerning this subject, few will listen. For the majority have made their ears heavy in order not to hear, just as Isaiah said.

For the minority, I will offer one example, and then conclude this book. If, my brothers, a certain king was out on a plain, seated upon a high throne, and before him were standing all of the highest ranking officers and, with fear and great trembling, all of the orders of soldiers—if, I say, that king was to order one of them to come before him in order to speak with him about a certain duty, and then some of the others, envying his boldness toward the king, tried to prohibit him from approaching, do you think he would listen to them and disregard the king? I believe that he would not even pay the slightest attention to them, but rather with great earnestness would run to the king, thinking this a great honor and distinction. So, if we would be so willingly obedient to a mortal king, why then should we not be even more willingly obedient to our heavenly King and Master? An earthly king can only deprive us of honor, glory, and possessions, which things, either today or tomorrow, death destroys. But, at the judgment, who will importune the God Who is able to condemn us to eternal death? What will we wretches who now transgress the Master's commandments do then, when the great judgment takes place? Do we think that we will then be able to make an excuse before God, Whom we now disregard, saying, "So-and-so prohibited us and so we did not execute Thy command?" Many of us will most likely say this, but to no avail.

For this reason we must repent now, before that hour comes. We must forsake the desires of the devil and the customs of men. We must perform the commandments of God, preparing ourselves with the proper preparation to partake frequently of the body and blood of our Lord Jesus Christ. And this, so that through divine

Communion we may be strengthened by the grace of God, and, thus strengthened, do every day the good and virtuous and perfect will of God on earth, as it is done in heaven by the angels. But if some prohibit us, we must beseech them as our Spiritual Fathers, with fervent tears in our eyes, until we wholly convince them to allow it, so that we may be deemed worthy to receive the pledge of the Spirit in our hearts with perfect assurance. May we be deemed worthy, both here and in God's kingdom, to glorify together with the angels and all the Saints the Father, and the Son, and the Holy Spirit, the Monad in Trinity and the Trinity in Unity, the infinitely perfect God, unto the everlasting ages of ages. Amen.

Portable Icon, 16th c., Holy Monastery of Grigoriou. Mount Athos.

Saint John Chrysostom

O Niptir, Katholicon, Holy Monastery of Stavronikita, Mount Athos.

Washing of the Disciples' Feet

Ye call ne Master and Lord: and ye say well; for so I am. If I then, your Lord and Master, have washed your feet; ye also ought to wash one another's feet. For I have given you an example, that ye should do as I have done to you.

Jn. 13:13-15

APPENDIX A

On What the Mystery of the Divine Eucharist Represents[225]

Consider that there are three things required to make a gift most precious: 1) that the gift itself be great, 2) that the person giving the gift have love, and 3) that the person receiving the gift be benefited by it. These three things are wondrously found in the Mystery of the divine Eucharist.

1. The Greatness of the Gift

First, consider the greatness of this gift, for indeed, God has bestowed upon us great things. He has granted us our own selves, creating us by bringing us out of nonbeing into being in His image and likeness. He granted us innumerable creations, heavenly and earthly, immaterial and material, unto our life and protection. He created heaven for us, and the earth, and all that is in them. But all of these gifts and charismata, even if they are in their own way very great and precious, are still finite and limited in power. However, by His incarnate economy God granted men an infinite gift and charisma, that of deification. This charisma, however, occurred directly only in the humanity of Jesus Christ, with which God the Word was united hypostatically, and it was by means of this union that this charisma, indirectly, came to us. Wherefore, there

---

225 Translator's note: This is the Twenty-Sixth Meditation from St. Nikodemos' book, *Pneumatika Gymnasmata* [*Spiritual Exercises*] ([Thessaloniki: Regopoulos, 1999], 213–221).

still remained something for our Lord to give us. Moreover, He desired to give Himself to each of the faithful individually, and in this way to bestow in a greater manner the infinite beneficence of His incarnation.[226]

And so that which was missing, behold, He grants and grants continuously by means of the Holy Communion of the Mysteries: all the riches and blessings of His all-holy body and precious blood, all the worth and virtues of His deified soul, and all the natural perfections of His Divinity. For this reason the divine John of Damaskos said: "This Mystery is called a 'receiving' (metalipsis) because through it we receive the Divinity of Jesus. And it is called 'Communion' because through it we enter into communion with Christ and are made partakers both of His flesh and of His Divinity."[227] In brief, this Mystery is an icon of the entire incarnate economy, according to Patriarch Jeremiah, and contains within it the birth of the Lord and His upbringing, His election, the passion, His death, His burial, His decent into Hades, the resurrection, the ascension, His enthronement at the right hand of the Father, and the second coming, just as the Divine Liturgies of Basil and Chrysostom demonstrate. What am I saying? Divine Communion is even an icon of the enjoyment and union of the blessed in the future age, as the divine Nicholas Cabasilas says.[228] Then, the blessed will be united with one another and with Christ, as the members of a body are united to their head. Indeed, even now, by partaking of the one bread and of the one cup we are united with one another and

---

226 Translator's note: Concerning the greatness of Holy Communion, St. Symeon of Thessaloniki writes:

> Communion, then, is the union of God with us. It is deification, sanctification, the fullness of grace, illumination, a defense against every adversary, and the provision of every good. And what else? It is a mixing and communion with God. It is the Mystery of Mysteries, the sanctification of the saints (and truly the Holy of Holies), the rite of all rites, and the chief and perfecter of all rites. For the only Author of sanctification, the Word, instituted Communion and handed it down, and He is Communion. He instituted it and gave it to us in order that He might be with us. (De Sacra Liturgia, PG 155, 253C).

227 *Fragmenta in Matthaeum* PG 96, 1409D.

228 Cf. *De Vita in Christo* 4 PG 150, 624D–625B; *The Life in Christ*, 146-148.

with Christ,[229] according to the prayer of the Lord, "that they may be one, even as We are one" (Jn. 17:22). None other of the seven Holy Mysteries includes all of these things. Wherefore, Dionysios the Areopagite named this Mystery the "rite of rites," as perfecting and embracing all of the other Mysteries.[230]

Thus, there is nothing more that we can ask from our Redeemer. We must just say along with Philip, "Lord... it sufficeth us" (Jn. 14:8). And if we were to ask for something more from Him in this present life, He could answer us: "My children, this Mystery I have granted you is the fullness of all blessings, and I do not have anything more to give you now, for I have granted you every blessing in the wheat and the wine," saying on our account that which Isaac said to Esau concerning his son Jacob: "With wheat and wine have I sustained him: and what shall I do now unto thee, my son?" (Gen. 27:37). O unsurpassable charisma! O incomparable gift, which will be incomprehensible to the many-eyed Cherubim and the six-winged Seraphim unto all ages!

Now, my brother, on account of the great liberality God shows towards you, should you not offer to God wholeheartedly the small liberty of your free will? On account of the great beneficence God has shown towards you by means of this Mystery, should you not also offer a sacrifice, to thank Him, offering your whole self, soul and body, to Him in order to serve Him? Suppose you have remained thankless until now, O ungrateful man, and have been inconsiderate towards all of the other spiritual gifts God has given you. Do you have such an ungrateful heart that you will still remain thankless towards a God Who gives His whole Self to you? What will the

---

229 Cf. 1 Cor. 10:16–17.

230 He says:

> For, as our celebrated teacher has declared (either Paul, that is, or Hierotheos), this is indeed the rite of rites... because the perfection of the other hierarchical symbols [that is, the other sacraments] is only achieved by way of the divine and perfecting Gifts. For scarcely any of the hierarchic rites can be performed without the most-divine Eucharist as the high point, divinely ministering the gathering to the One of the person participating in the rite; and, by the gift of the perfecting Mysteries handed down by God, his communion with God is in fact perfected. (*De Ecclesiastica Hierarchia* 3.1, PG 424C–424D; *Pseudo-Dionysius: The Complete Works*, 209).

angels say about your great ingratitude? What will all the Saints of heaven say, who know well the extreme liberality of Christ and the extreme stinginess of your soul, about your great inconsideration? You should be ashamed, my brother, ashamed that you show such thanklessness toward a Mystery which is named "Thanksgiving" [Eucharist]. And it is called this, not only because the Lord offered it with thanksgiving, as it is written—"Jesus took bread, and blessed it... And He took the cup, and gave thanks" (Mt. 26:26–27)—but also because its very name prompts us to give thanks to God for the many blessings and graces He has given us through this Mystery, which is of the greatest importance, as Cyril of Alexandria says, and especially the divine Chrysostom: "The best preservative of any blessing is the remembrance of the blessing, and continual thanksgiving."[231] Remember that according to the measure of blessings you receive will be the measure of your punishments, if you misuse these blessings. That is, the greater the blessings are which you receive from God, the greater the punishment you will receive if you do not use them in a proper manner.[232] Make a promise to give your whole self to the Lord, for He gives His whole Self to

---

231 *On Matthew* 25.3, PG 57, 331; NPNF (V1-10), 170. Wherefore, the sacred Nicholas Cabasilas, Bishop of Dyrrachios, also says:

> There is one more question to be considered. Since the sacrifice is both eucharistic and supplicatory, why does it not bear both names? Why is it simply called the Eucharist? It is because it takes its name from the more important element. Our reasons for thanksgiving are more numerous than those for supplication, since the number of benefits which we have received exceeds that of which we still have need; the latter are only a part, the former are the whole. The benefits we ask for are simply a part of what we have obtained already. (*Sacrae Liturgiae Interpretatio* 52, PG 150, 485B; trans. *A Commentary on the Divine Liturgy*, 116)

Furthermore, the divine Chrysostom says: "For this reason the dread Mysteries are called Eucharist [Thanksgiving], because they are the remembrance of the many blessings of God, and they signify the very sum of God's providence, and by every means they work upon us to give thanks" (*On Matthew* 25.3, PG 57, 331; NPNF [V1-10], 170).

232 Translator's note: For according to St. Gregory of Nyssa: "As each shall receive his wages, just as the Apostle says (cf. 1 Cor. 3:14), according to his labor, so also shall each receive punishment according to the extent of his negligence" (*Contra Eunomium* 12, PG 45, 912C).

you. Thank Him from your heart for granting you such a great and exceeding gift, and ask Him to add a new spirit and a new heart to the many blessings He has given you, so that you may reckon His blessings properly and offer them back with the proper thanksgiving and reciprocation, both through words and works: "A new heart also will I give you, and a new spirit will I put within you… and cause you to walk in My statutes, and ye shall keep My judgments, and do them" (Ezek. 36:26–27).

2. The love of the person giving the gift

Consider, my brother, the love with which Jesus Christ gives you the gift of divine Communion. For in love is to be found the entirety of every benefaction, and love is like the soul of a gift, while the gift is like the body. Now the love of Christ that caused Him to give us this Mystery reached the furthest end and perfection, as the Evangelist John says: "Having loved His own which were in the world, He loved them unto the end" (Jn. 13:1). And just as the heat of a furnace is recognizable on account of the visible flames that come from it, in like manner is the infinite love of Christ recognizable from the following three things: 1) the time when He instituted the Mystery, 2) the manner in which He instituted it, and 3) the difficulties overcome by this institution. The time was that evening of Great and Holy Thursday, when the traitor Judas was planning on betraying Jesus and the whole council of the Jews was planning on putting Him to a most heinous death. And when He decided to give the bread of life to men, it was then that those ingrates were scheming more than ever to remove Him from life and put Him to death. For this reason the Evangelist said: "Now when the evening was come, He sat down with the twelve…. And as they were eating, Jesus took bread, and blessed it, and brake it, and gave it to the disciples…. And He took the cup, and gave thanks, and gave it to them" (Mt. 26:20, 26–27). The manner in which He gave Communion to us is in the form of bread and wine, which is to say, in the form of food and drink. And not food and drink that are hard to find, but that are found in nearly every place where men are found. This is for two reasons. First, so that the Lord could become a part of us to such an extent that, just as there cannot be found any technique and method which can separate from our hypostasis food which, just a short while ago, was mixed with and changed into our body; in the same way, there would not be found any technique or any power which could separate us from the Lord. Second, so that we could easily and whenever we want receive Communion and become one with the Lord, in that it is easy to find bread and wine.[233]

More than anything else, the Lord's love is made manifest in the difficulties He overcame in order to benefit us with this Mystery. For, although the Lord foresaw the infinite multitude of His priests and Christian people that would show such irreverence, disdain, tepidity (or rather, coldness), and thousands of other sacrileges towards His all-holy body and blood, His love nevertheless conquered all of these difficulties and obstacles: "For many waters cannot quench love, neither can the floods drown it" (S. of S. 8:7). His love, I say, conquered all of this, and He condescended to

---

233 Some add a third reason for which God wanted to become food for us. This is because children distribute their love between the mother who gave them birth and the rearer or nurse who feeds them. Wherefore the Son of God, so that our love would not be divided, not only gave us birth through Baptism and so became our Mother, but also wanted to feed us with His body and His blood, and so became also our Nurse, as the divine Chrysostom so eloquently put it: "He Who became our Mother was not ashamed to become our Nurse" (cf. *In Psalmum 50*.6, PG 55, 572). And there is a fourth reason for which the Lord wanted to become food for us, namely, self-love, because of which each person by nature loves himself. In order for man's love not to be divided between love for himself and love for God, but so that all of it might be offered to God, this manner was found, He giving us His body and His blood as food. This food is not changed into our body and blood in the same way as other foods which we eat, but rather, being the body and blood of our Lord Who is perfect God and perfect man, this more potent food is spiritually changed into our soul and body, that is, our whole self is changed into it and it makes our soul and body, by grace, Christ's body and soul, as Paul says: "We are members of His body, of His flesh, and of His bones" (Eph. 5:30). For it is natural that the more potent and powerful things conquer and change into themselves those things that are less potent and weaker, as this is most wisely demonstrated by the wise Nicholas Cabasilas in the fourth chapter of his work, *On the Life in Christ* (cf. PG 150, 593B–593C; *The Life in Christ*, 122-123). For this reason, while we love our self, we love the Lord at the same time, Who is our self. Rather, loving the Lord, it follows that we love our self, which is the Lord's.

endure everything, just so that He might be able to become one with our souls. And what is more, to His patience He added desire, and the most extreme of desires, desiring with all of His heart and all of His soul to unite with us even in the hour before His passion, for which reason He said: "With desire I have desired to eat this passover with you before I suffer" (Lk. 22:15). All of the Forefathers and Prophets, all the nations, and all men anticipated and desired, for five and a half thousand years, His coming into the world and incarnation. Now, He desires to come into our hearts by means of this Mystery, and, somehow, He constrains Himself into the Mystery, with a desire worthy only of His divine heart and His own Divinity. O truly most God-befitting and invincible love! Or rather, O flames of love which have arisen even to heaven, as it is written: "Love is strong as death… her shafts are shafts of fire, even the flames thereof!" (S. of S. 8:6). Who could ever comprehend such extravagances of God's love if faith did not reveal them to us?

But alas! How do you respond, my brother, to such love from your Lord? Whence arose in you such contrary actions? How is it that God so greatly desires to unite with your wretched soul, and you, on the contrary, so little desire to unite with Him, Who is the most supreme good? How is it that God displays such tender warmth towards you, and you, who are but clay, display such coldness towards Him? How is it that God deigns to seek to come and dwell in your heart by means of this Mystery, in order to enlighten you, in order to sanctify you; and you, the thankless creature, shut the door and do not allow Him to enter in? Woe to you, my beloved! Do you any longer have a single right not to serve and be thankful toward such an excessive divine love, but to serve and indulge your passions? Do you any longer have a right to turn back to Egypt with your heart and to desire, like that thankless Hebrew people, the leeks, garlic, and onions of Egypt—that is, the hedonistic pleasures of your senses and your carnal appetites—after you have received that divine manna as your food?[234] What else must Christ do in order to overcome your great hardness and inhumanity, besides destroying you and casting your bones into

---

234 Cf. Num. 11:4–5.

Hades, as He strew the bones of the Hebrews in the wilderness, as it is written: "But with whom was He grieved forty years? Was it not with them that had sinned, whose carcasses fell in the wilderness?" (Heb. 3:5).

For this reason, come before the divine majesty and openly confess your inhumanity, abhor it with all of your heart, and detest it many times over. Offer yourself completely to God through this Mystery, receiving Communion because of love and with love for the beloved Jesus, Who out of His extreme love for you instituted this beloved Mystery in order that there may be that greatly beloved and heavenly union between the loving God and you, His beloved, as we previously said.[235] And from now on, brother, awaken, and cause yourself to fear with an extreme horror and terror every sin and every pollution of the flesh and spirit, saying this to yourself: "I have now become a dwelling place of God through partaking of the immaculate Mysteries, so how can I possibly become a dwelling place of sin? I have been united to Christ and have become one of His members, so how can I any longer make the members of Christ the members of a harlot and of the devil? 'Shall I then take the members of Christ, and make them the members of an harlot? God forbid' (1 Cor. 6:15)." Last of all, beseech the Lord, in Whom, because of Whom, and Whom you believe, hope, and love to give you grace so that you may render Him love for love, eros for eros, and warmth for warmth, without ever being afraid of or conquered by any difficulty brought by the enemy on the way, attempting to discourage you—just as the Lord was not overcome by any difficulty when benefiting you. And just as He is sacrificed daily on the Holy Table because of His love for you, so you are obligated to offer Him four sacrifices because of your love for Him: 1) You must offer the sacrifice of all of your thoughts, and of your will, and of your way of thinking: that is, you must humble yourself before Him and sacrifice all of your notions and desires.

---

235 "If a body is changed in its activity from contact with another body, then how can he remain unchanged who touches the body of God with innocent hands?" says John of the Ladder (Step 28, PG 88, 1137C–1137D; trans. *The Ladder of Divine Ascent* [Boston: Holy Transfiguration Monastery, 2001], 219).

Concerning this, it is written: "A sacrifice unto God is a broken spirit" (Ps. 50:17). 2) You are to offer Him the sacrifice of your words, glorifying and thanking Him always for the love He shows to you in this Mystery: "Sacrifice unto God a sacrifice of praise" (Ps. 49:15). 3) You must offer Him a sacrifice through works, doing charitable acts of mercy, offering hospitality, and doing other such good works, as it is written: "But to do good and to share forget not: for with such sacrifices God is well pleased" (Heb. 13:16). 4) The last sacrifice you are to offer is your body, sacrificing for God all of your carnal passions and appetites, just as the Apostle orders you, saying: "I beseech you therefore, brethren, by the mercies of God, that ye present your bodies a living sacrifice, holy, acceptable unto God" (Rom. 12:1).[236] Know that, according to

---

236 Translator's note: Let us also heed the words of St. Symeon the New Theologian: Christ came granting deliverance from and annulment of sins to those who would believe in Him—deliverance through Baptism and annulment through His food and drink, for He says: "He that eateth My flesh, and drinketh My blood, dwelleth in Me, and I in him" (Jn. 6:56), and the one who dwells in Him bears fruit, not corruption. So then, he who does not bear fruit after Baptism and after communing with Christ is cut down and thrown into the fire as a fruitless tree. For not only is he who is defiled in flesh and spirit, and thus approaches the Holy Things unworthily, subject to severe judgment—for approaching thus, he becomes guilty of the body and blood of the Lord (cf. 1 Cor. 11:27)—but also whoever eats and drinks heedlessly and in vain by not keeping the remembrance of Christ, Who died and rose for us, so long as he dishonorably and vainly negates such a great good. And by approaching such a great Mystery thanklessly, he is guilty of idleness, inasmuch as the Lord will not even spare from judgment those who speak an idle word (cf. Mt. 12:36). For he who approaches the body and blood of Christ with remembrance of Him Who died and rose for us must not only be pure of every defilement of flesh and spirit (so that he does not partake unto condemnation), but also must actively show that he remembers Him Who died and rose for our sake, through his having died to sin, to the world, and to himself, and by living unto God in Christ Jesus our Lord. But he who does not bear fruit, working rather corruption and wickedness, will be relegated to the place of the unbaptized, the unbelievers, and the impious, concerning whom the blessed Apostle says: "Of how much sorer punishment, suppose ye, shall he be thought worthy, who hath trodden under foot the Son of God, and hath counted the blood of the covenant, wherewith he was sanctified, an unholy thing" (Heb. 10:29). (*Alphabetika Kephalaia* [*Alphabetical Chapters*] [Hagion Oros: I.M. Stavronikita, 2005], ch. 2, 58–60)

the moral philosophers, the creative force of love is similitude—according to the saying, "similitude, attraction."[237] Rather, love is again the cause of love, and whoever wishes to be loved must himself love. Wherefore, Wisdom says, "I love them that love me" (Pr. 8:17). And the beloved disciple says, "We love Him, because He first loved us" (1 Jn. 4:19).

3. The benefit enjoyed by the person receiving the gift

Consider, brother, the benefit you enjoy from this gift of the Eucharist, which is called Communion, as we have previously said, in order to show us that it makes all the good things and the kingdom of Jesus Christ to be common with our soul. For this reason St. Isidore Pelousiotes says, "The reception of the divine Mysteries is called Communion on account of the union with Christ that it grants us, and because it causes us to become communicants of His kingdom."[238] Wherefore, that infinite sum and collection of blessings and glory which Jesus gathered into Himself by His life and His death, He gives to us totally and completely in this great Mystery, by means of which the Lord seeks to renew in each person individually the effects and benefit that His divine passion brought to all the world. By this Mystery, He not only shows that He does not think it a great thing that He labored and suffered for our salvation one time, with just one body, but shows how He again desires to suffer for us. For this reason He wishes to multiply, sacramentally, the very same body innumerable times, so that it may be present on each altar, and He wishes to receive in that body, sacramentally, all of His sufferings, in order thus to multiply our own benefit, again and again, innumerable times: "In every place incense shall be offered unto My Name, and a pure offering" (Mal. 1:11).

The Lord could have benefited us and given us His grace by means of His creations, as He does in the other Mysteries. But in this Mystery He is found essentially,[239] and He wishes to give it

---

237 Aristotle, *Nicomachean Ethics*, 1159b3.
238 *Liber* 1, *Epistola* 228, PG 78, 325A.
239 Cf. Eutychios of Constantinople, *Sermo de Paschate et de Sacrosancta Eucharistia 3*, PG 86², 2393D–2396A.

to us and benefit us with His own hand, illumining our intellect, warming our heart, mortifying our passions, strengthening our weaknesses, preserving our health, and restoring our senses to their proper order. These benefits are most clearly described for us by the eloquent mouths of the theologians, two of whom are sufficient to bear witness to them. Gregory the Theologian says:

> When the most sacred body of Christ is received and eaten in a proper manner, it becomes a weapon against those who war against us, returns those to God who had left Him, strengthens the weak, causes those who are healthy to be glad, heals sicknesses, and preserves health. Through it we become meek and more willing to accept correction, more longsuffering in our pains, more fervent in our love, more detailed in our knowledge, more willing to do obedience, and keener in the workings of the charismata.[240]

And Cyril of Alexandria says: "Christ pacifies and calms the fierce war of the flesh, ignites piety towards God, and deadens the passions."[241] And I will say something greater still. Just as grubs and silk worms leave seeds in the trees or in the earth that remain there

---

240 Translator's note: This quote is taken from Gennadios Scholarios (*De Sacramentali Corpore Christi* 1, PG 160, 357A), who himself says he is quoting "the divine Gregory."

241 *In Joannis Evangelium* 4.2, PG 73, 585A. And the divine Chrysostom says:

> For if a man who has worms feeding on his entrails is not even able to breathe because his inward parts are all wasting away, how shall we, having so large a serpent eating us all up inside (it is anger I mean), how, I say, shall we be able to produce anything noble? How then are we to be freed from this pest? If we drink a potion that is able to kill the worms within us and the serpents. "And of what nature," it will be asked, "may this potion be, that has such power?" The blood of Christ, if it be received with full assurance; for this will have power to extinguish every disease. (*On Matthew* 4.9, PG 57, 50; NPNF [V1-10], 25–26).

> What am I saying? The very demons against their will confess the benefit of divine Communion. For when St. John Bostrinos, a man having authority over unclean spirits, asked them which things they fear most, they replied that they feared Baptism, the Cross, and divine Communion. When they were asked which of these three they feared the most, they said: "If you guarded well that of which you partook, none of us could ever harm a Christian" (from the third hypothesis compiled by John of Antioch).

during the winter, and then the gentle spring comes and opens the seeds and they come alive; so the Lord, being united to us in this world through Communion, leaves seeds of immortality in our heavy and earthly body. By means of these implanted seeds the body will be resurrected at the end of the world unto eternal life, just as the Lord described it: "And I will raise him up at the last day" (Jn. 6:54).[242] O my God, may Thy Holy Name be glorified countless times, for Thou madest such a great provision in order to benefit us by this Mystery!

So my beloved brother, what do you say now, after hearing these things? If the Lord of all gave you every good thing through His body and blood, what is there that you still cannot give Him? If the Lord benefited you so much with this Mystery, do you still have such a heart so as to wrong Him with more sins? Woe to you! If the Lord were to but a single time give this most greatly beneficial Mystery to one of the highest spirits of heaven (in the same way as we receive it), that spirit would not think it sufficient thanks to be destroyed and return to nothingness out of love for its God. But you, the rotten worm, who have received so many times that heavenly gift, you who have confessed and rejected your sins prior to receiving Communion, straightway after communing revert to your old ways like a dog returns to its vomit,[243] and you plot treacherously against your God with new sins! O what thanklessness! Is this how you express your love? Is this the thanks you ought to show to your Benefactor? Is this the benefit you receive from the Mystery? You ought to be embarrassed, brother, by your wretchedness, and you should be ashamed that you have taken such little fruit and benefit from that divine and most beneficial Table, constantly desiring the hedonistic pleasures of the flesh and the goods the world can give you: "Be ashamed and confounded for your own ways, O house of Israel" (Ezek. 36:32). Be resolved to prepare yourself next time with greater care and earnestness, so that you may receive Communion

---

242 Translator's note: Cf. Cyril of Alexandria: "By His own flesh, our Lord hides the life in us and puts in us a kind of seed of incorruptibility, which destroys all the corruption which is in us" (*In Joannis Evangelium* 4.2, PG 73, 581C).

243 Cf. 2 Pet. 2:22.

having confessed fervently, with contrition, having fulfilled your ascetical rule, and having fasted and watched over your thoughts (as much as possible), "with the fear of God, with faith, and with love," just as the priest calls out to you. This way you will serve the Lord and take greater benefit and fruit from the divine Mysteries. This is because, according to the greater or lesser preparation a man performs, so does he receive greater or lesser grace from the divine Mysteries.

It is obvious that the more frequently you prepare yourself and commune, the more frequently your soul receives benefit from the Mysteries, receiving them unto the healing of soul and body, unto the remission of sins, unto the further reception of His divine grace, unto the mortification of the passions, and unto the keeping of the commandments of Christ. For this reason, the divine Apostles in their Canons[244] and the divine Fathers in their liturgies and teachings with one voice urge all Christians—both monastics and laypeople—who do not have an impediment from their Spiritual Fathers to prepare themselves in the manner we just described, and frequently partake of the divine Mysteries. For the longer they put this off and do not receive Communion, the more they are ruled by passions and sins. Last of all, thank the Lord Who has endured your great thanklessness for so long, and beseech Him from now on to overpower it by His grace. And thank Him because He subjected Himself to such baseness (if I may use this expression) in order to become food for you, and wrought such a great wonder for your benefit. Thank Him Who now works this wonder of turning you entirely into Himself and into His love, deeming you worthy to receive frequently in a fitting manner His own holiness, His own purity, and His own beauty, so that you also may become completely holy, completely pure, and completely beautiful in soul and body (for, in a natural manner, man becomes what he eats, and for this reason it is the opinion of historians that the rabbits which dwell in the high mountains are completely white, for they do not eat anything else but the white snow)—so that, becoming these things,

---

244 Canons 8 and 9 (*Pedalion*, 11–13; *The Rudder*, 20–21).

you may hear from the Bridegroom Christ those words of the Song: "Thou art all fair, my love; there is no spot in thee" (S. of S. 4:7).[245]

Eighth Reading[246]

...You must resolutely do the following for God: You must remember the passion of your Redeemer, Jesus Christ. You must always thank God for His blessings, humble yourself, and obey His law and His commandments. You must reverence the All-holy Mother of God and all of His Saints. You must attend and visit the churches of Christ. You must stand with fear and piety during the dread Sacrifice of the Liturgy. But, above all, you must set your gaze upon two things which will most of all help you to remain in a good state. One is to frequently partake of the divine Mysteries with the proper preparation of confession, contrition, the fulfillment of your rule, and fasting as much as you are able. The other is prayer.

Concerning the role of the divine Mysteries, we have here only this to say to you: Just as God planted the tree of life in the earthly Paradise, so He planted in the Paradise of the Church another incomparably more precious tree of life, the Mystery of the divine Eucharist. But just as Adam, in order to sustain the life of his body, did not eat only rarely of the fruit of that tree of life, but it was necessary for him to frequently partake of it in order to live, so it is for you, brother, in order for you to sustain the spiritual life. It is not sufficient for you to approach rarely, every two or three months, to receive the Master Christ. Rather, you must approach frequently (according to the strength of your spiritual state and the advice of your Spiritual Father). And I assure you that through your own experience you will come to understand just how wondrous are the effects of divine Communion when you frequently commune with the necessary preparation and piety. Bees live longer than any

---

245 See also the end of the last [Eighth] Reading in this book, *Pneumatika Gymnasmata* (458–459), where I speak again about the divine Eucharist.

246 Translator's note: Since St. Nikodemos refers us to the end of the Eighth Reading of his book, where he again speaks about the Eucharist, we have included here those words as well.

of the flies, wasps, or so-called insects, because they feed daily on honey. The rabbits that live in the high mountains of the Alps are white because they are almost always standing in the snow and continuously eat it, as we mentioned previously in the Meditation on the divine Eucharist. Many birds of the eastern Molucca Islands do not stink when they die, neither do their bodies rot, because they eat the savory and fragrant fruits of the region. For this reason, because the devil knows all too well these good things which we receive from frequent Communion, that hater of good diligently attempts to block us from this food of Paradise in order to deprive us of these things and in this manner make us weak, so as to conquer us without a fight—just as Holofernes attempted to defeat the city of Bethulia, the fatherland of the wise Judith, without any struggle, by cutting off the water mains which brought water into the city from the outside and thus preventing the city from being irrigated any longer by the springs around it.[247]

247 Cf. Judith 7:1–32.

ΛΑΒΕΤΕ ΦΑΓΕΤΕ ΤΜ
ΕΠΤ ϹΩΜΑ·

ΙϹ ΧϹ

Katholikon, Holy Monastery of Stavronikita, Mount Athos.

The Communion of the Apostles

Verily, verily, I say unto you, Except ye eat the flesh of the Son of man, and drink his blood, ye have no life in you. Whose eateth my flesh, and drinketh my blood, hath eternal life, and I will raise him up at the last day. For my flesh is meat indeed, and my blood is drink indeed. He that eateth my flesh, and drinketh my blood, dwelleth in me, and I in him.

Jn. 6:52-56

APPENDIX B

Concerning the Mystery of the Divine Eucharist[248]

Some slander us and say that we believe the Mystery of the divine Eucharist, that is, the immaculate body and precious blood of the Lord, to be passible and subject to corruption, and that the whole body of the Lord is not in every part of the sanctified bread, nor the whole blood in every part of the sanctified wine. But those who say such things are ridiculous. For they should have read the prayers we composed and arranged in stanzas, dedicated to our Lord Jesus, which were published in the year 1796 in our book *Aoratos Polemos* [*Unseen Warfare*]. Then they would have learned what we believe concerning this subject. But, because they have become blind and have not read those prayers, we present here verbatim what we wrote there concerning this subject, unto the everlasting shame of those who unjustly criticize us.

We write the following on page 334 of the aforementioned book:

Revealing a mystery to initiates, O my Jesus, Thou didst leave a pledge for a mortal race, changing the bread into Thy very body

248 Translator's note: This is part of St. Nikodemos' personal *Apologia*, entitled *Homologia Pisteos* [*Confession of Faith*] (Venice: 1819), and called by Dr. George Bebis "St. Nicodemos' most important work" (*A Handbook of Spiritual Counsel*, 20). The entire text of the *Confession of Faith* can be found in the book, *En Askesei kai Martyrio* [*In Asceticism and Martyrdom*] (P. B. Paschos [Athens: Harmos, 1996], 105–181). This excerpt is from pp. 166–177 of that book. See the forthcoming third volume in this present series, due out in 2007.

at the supper, and the wine into Thy very blood, and Thou didst command them to do this in Thy memory. And I am sanctified by frequently partaking of these, which are incorruptible, and being deified I cry to Thee....

And further down, on page 335, we write the following: "Jesus, the One wholly in the whole Mystery and wholly present in every part of it, I confess to Thee that I approach Thy Holy Table without the necessary preparation." Behold the pious mindset we have concerning this incomprehensible Mystery. And we not only believed, and do believe, these things, but wrote them with our very own hand. And we not only wrote these things, but printed and published them, not one year ago, or two, or three, but over ten years ago, as if we foresaw how some envious people would rise up against us to slander us. So we anticipated these things and have shut their babbling mouths with these words. And even though they are but brief words, they are sufficient to muzzle those slanderers, as they contain the whole spike and brunt of the refutation to their slanders, if I may put it in this way.

However, in order to place a bridle on their lips, behold what we add further, in abundance:

To better understand and summarize what has been said, and in order to show what we believe about this Mystery, we refer here all of the constitutive distinctions and characteristics of the divine Mystery of the Eucharist into two general and universal definitions, from which all the others can be derived.

We believe unquestioningly with our heart, and we confess with our mouth unto salvation, and we write with our hand to further convey that: First, the all-immaculate body of the Lord and His life-giving blood are actual; and second, they are spiritual. They are actual because the bread set forth on the Holy Table is, after the sanctification, truly the body of our Lord Jesus Christ, which is not a different body now than it was then, but the same. Likewise, the wine in the chalice is, after the sanctification, truly the life-giving blood of the Lord, which is not a different blood now than it was then, but the same. And because there is not one body and then another, but actually one and the same, it follows that the sanctified bread is the body of the Lord—the body actually conceived of the Holy Spirit, the one actually born of the Virgin, the one actually baptized, the one which actually suffered, the one which was actually crucified, the one which was actually buried, the one which actually resurrected, the one which actually ascended into the heavens, the one which is actually seated at the right hand of the Father, and the one which will actually come to judge the living and the dead.[249]

Wherefore, Meletios Syrigos said:

> In our Holy Liturgy we remember the entire economy of Christ, remembering and hymning with a voice of praise His birth, His preaching of the Gospel, the holy passion, the Cross, the taking-down from the Cross, the third-day resurrection, and the ascension into the heavens. Yet all of these things we do over the bread which is set forth.

And in the 17th chapter of the two Councils convened against Cyril Loukaris, in Constantinople and in Jassy, the following is written:

> In the Sacred Rite we believe that our Lord Jesus Christ is truly and actually present. So, after the sanctification of the bread and the wine, the bread is changed, transubstantiated, converted, transformed, into the true body of the Lord, which was born in Bethlehem of the Virgin and Theotokos Mary; which was baptized in the Jordan; which suffered; which was buried, resurrected, ascended, and is seated at the right hand of the Father; and which will come upon the clouds of heaven. And the wine that is converted and transubstantiated into the true blood of the Lord is the very blood which was shed for the life of the world by the Lord when He was suspended upon the Cross.

From this it also follows that the Mystery of the Eucharist is a true sacrifice and a perfect offering, in which Christ Himself is both

---

249 Cf. Nicholas Cabasilas, *Sacrae Liturgiae Interpretatio* 27, PG 150, 425C-425D; *A Commentary on the Divine Liturgy*, 70.

the Sacrificer and the Sacrificed, and the Receiver of the sacrifice together with the Father. He is the Priest and the sacrificial Victim, the One Who offers and is offered and for Whom the offering is accomplished. Wherefore St. John Chrysostom said: "As then while offered (Christ) in many places, He is one body and not many bodies; so also is He one sacrifice. He is our High Priest, Who offered the sacrifice that cleanses us. That sacrifice we also offer now, which was then offered, and which cannot be exhausted."[250]

The body and blood of the Lord in the Mystery are also spiritual. For even though they are actual and true (as we said above), they are not, however, physical, or visible, or wholly sensible, but they are spiritual. This is understood in two ways. First, in that the body and blood of the Lord in the Mystery are acted upon and sanctified, not by any natural physical means, but by the almighty energy and power of the All-holy and Perfecting Spirit. Hence, this Mystery is supranatural. It is sacramental. It is incomprehensible. And it follows that it is beyond words and inexplicable and is accepted only by faith.

Second, the body and blood of the Lord in the Eucharist are spiritual insofar as they are not perceived according to the mode of the human body, but according to the mode of the soul, which is spirit, as Meletios Syrigos says. From this it follows that, just as the spirit, that is, the soul, is invisible and not discernable by the senses, so also the body and blood of the Lord in the Eucharist are invisible and not discernable by the senses, being beyond the senses. For the same Meletios Syrigos says: "Neither do we believe that the body of the Lord is visible and entirely sensible throughout, but we say that it is hidden beneath the covering of the bread, and that it is invisibly present in the Eucharist."[251] Wherefore some abuse

---

250 *On Hebrews* 17.3, PG 63, 131; NPNF (V1-14), 449. Concerning this, see also *Dodekabiblos* 807.

251 Translator's note: St. Cyril of Jerusalem says: "For the body is given to you in the form of bread, and the blood is given to you in the form of wine" (*Mystagogiae* 4.3, SC 126, 136; NPNF [V2-07], 151). And St. Nicholas Cabasilas says: "It is the body of Christ which is the substance which lies beneath the appearance of bread" (*Sacrae Liturgiae Interpretatio* 32, PG 150, 440D; trans. *A Commentary on the Divine Liturgy*, 81). According to St. Ephraim the

the term "actual," wanting a sensible slaughtering of a body, and a sensible spilling of blood in the Mystery of the Eucharist. But if this were the case, we would also have to visibly bring in all of the sensible instruments used in this slaughter and in this spilling of the blood of the Lord, namely, the Cross, and the nails, and the spear, and the rest. But this is not the case, it is not so. For even if the sacrifice of the body of the Lord in the Mystery is actual, it is also spiritual, that is to say, it is mystical, invisible, and beyond the senses, wherefore it is also called a bloodless sacrifice. For the Mysteries demand faith, not the senses.[252]

From this it follows that just as the spirit, that is, the soul, is wholly present in the whole body, and wholly present in every part of the body, so also in the Eucharist is the body wholly present in the whole bread, and wholly present in every part of the bread. The same is to be said of the blood, which is wholly present in the whole wine, and wholly present in every part of the wine. From this it follows that just as the spirit, that is, the soul, remains incorrupt after the corruption of the body, likewise the body and blood of the Lord remain incorrupt after the corruption of the bread and

---

Syrian: "The body was the veil of Thy splendor... and the bread is the veil of the Fire that indwells it" (*Hymnem de Fide* 19.2-3, CSCO 154, 72; trans. Hieromonk Alexander Golitzin, *Et Introibo ad Altare Dei* [Thessaloniki: Patriarchikon Hidryma Paterikon Meleton, 1994], 367). St. Gregory Palamas says the same: "For this bread is like a veil concealing the Divinity within" (Homily 56, *Hellenes Pateres tes Ekklisias* [*Greek Fathers of the Church*], vol. 11 [Thessaloniki: Gregorios O Palamas, 1986], 406).

252 Translator's note: According to St. Cyril of Jerusalem:

> Be careful so as not to consider them as mere bread and wine, for they are the body and blood of Christ according to the received declaration of the Master. For even if the senses suggest this to you, yet let faith assure you. Judge not the matter from taste, but from faith be unquestioningly convinced that you have been deemed worthy of the body and blood of Christ. (*Mystagogiae* 4.6, SC 126, 138; NPNF [V2-07], 152).

And St. John Chrysostom says: "It is called a 'Mystery' because we do not believe what we see; for we see one thing, but believe another. Such is the nature of our Mysteries.... I do not judge what is apparent by sight, but by the eyes of the mind" (*On 1 Corinthians* 7.1, PG 61, 55; NPNF [V1-12], 34). St. Ambrose of Milan says the same thing: "We must not look at the things which are seen, but at the things which are not seen.... Believe, therefore, that the presence of the Divinity is there" (*De Mysteriis* 3.8, SC 25[bis], 158, 160; NPNF [V2-10], 318).

the wine. From this it follows that just as the spirit, that is, the soul, being one, is divided indivisibly into all of the members and parts of the body, and is distributed undividedly, in the same manner the body and blood in the Eucharist are divided indivisibly into all the parts of the bread and the wine, and are distributed undividedly. Wherefore it is said: "Broken but not divided; forever eaten, yet never consumed."[253]

Hence, in the year 1195, during the reign of the Emperor Alexios, the brother of Isaakios, a certain monk named Sikyditos asked, "So is the body of Christ incorruptible in the Mystery, just as it was after the passion and the resurrection, or is it corruptible, just as it was before His passion and death?" Following this, I say, those of a correct mindset brought forth testimonies from Cyril, Chrysostom, Gregory of Nyssa, and Eutychios of Constantinople: "The body of Christ in the Mystery is incorruptible, because it is that post-resurrection impassible body, not the pre-passion passible one. And whoever receives a part of the bread, receives the whole Christ,[254] and, in a strange manner, partakes of the divine Theurgy unto life eternal." Moreover, they brought forward examples from the abovementioned Eutychios, saying:

> Even if someone only receives a part of these, he wholly receives the whole holy body and precious blood of the

---

253 Translator's note: These are the words said by the bishop or priest in the Divine Liturgy when fracturing the sanctified bread (the body of the Lord) just before preparing the gifts for Holy Communion.

254 Notice that they say how one "receives the whole Christ," showing that those who commune in the Mysteries receive the whole Christ, the divinity and the humanity, and the soul and the body. That is to say, they receive the perfect God and the perfect man, because Christ is both perfect God and perfect man, according to John of Damaskos and all the sacred theologians. [Translator's note: That "the whole Christ" is present in the smallest particle of the sanctified bread is also attested to by St. Symeon the New Theologian: "You should suspect nothing physical, nor conceive anything earthly, but instead see this bread with spiritual eyes, and see that this little particle is made divine, and has become altogether like the bread which came down from heaven, which is true God, both the bread and drink of immortal life... the whole Christ Himself" (*Ethical Discourses* 3, SC 122, 428; trans. *On the Mystical Life*, vol. 1, 133, 134).]

Lord, for it is distributed undividedly throughout on account of the immixture. It is just as a seal, the impression of which is imparted to everything that receives it, while the seal itself remains of the same quality and is unaltered, even if a great number of items are sealed (that is, even though the impressions are many, the seal remains one and is not many). Or it is as a voice, which goes out and is dispersed into the air: it is whole before it is expelled, it remains whole in the air, and it is deposited in all who hear it, no hearer receiving more or less than the others. Rather, it is wholly indivisible and complete and real in the judgment of all, even if the hearers are thousands in number or greater.[255]

And Samonas of Gaza[256] and Gennadios Scholarios[257] liken the body of the Lord in the Mystery to a most understandable model, a mirror. For just as the whole sun appears in an intact and unshattered mirror, and also in every piece of a shattered mirror, in like manner the whole body of the Lord is present in the whole, unfractured bread, and also in every piece of the fractured bread. The same Samonas says:

> When the sanctified bread (which is the all-holy body of Christ) is fractured into pieces, do not consider the immaculate body to be divided, broken up, or disunited, for it is immortal, incorruptible, and never exhausted. But, rather, believe that after the sanctification there is a division of only that which is sensible, unto the strengthening of faith; for a present, visible sign of the things to come; and as a pledge of and provision for life eternal.[258]

And the divine Chrysostom says: "Let us now then draw near with faith (to the mystical Eucharist, that is), all who have an infirmity. For if they that touched the hem of His garment drew from Him

---

255 *Sermo de Paschate et de Eucharistia* 2, PG 86², 2393C. See *Dodekabiblos*, 807.

256 Cf. *De Sacramento Altaris*, PG 120, 832A.

257 Cf. *De Sacramentali Corpore Christi* 1, PG 160, 365B.

258 From the *Sacred Catechism*; *De Sacramento Altaris*, PG 120, 832C.

so much power, how much more they that wholly possess Him?"[259]
And John of Damaskos says in the prayer before Communion:
"And I, deplorable though I be, dare to receive Thy whole Body;
may I not be consumed."[260]

We also add this, that in addition to the other slanders, those
slander-loving brethren also accuse us of this, namely, that we carry
around with us under our hat an *artophorion*[261] containing the holy
bread, and that wherever we wish, whether on the road or somewhere
else, we sit down and commune. When we heard these obvious and
transparent slanders for the first time, we could not help but laugh;
or, rather, we derided their hatred for the brethren. For we have
every liberty, if we examine ourselves in accordance with the words
of the Apostle,[262] having thus prepared, to enter at any time into the
Temple of God and receive Communion from the priest. So what
need do we have to carry around a holy *artophorion*? Let those haters
of the brethren be sated from their slanders against us. The Judge
is near, to Whom they will have to give account concerning their
schemes against us, their fabricating of things which do not exist.

All these things we confess and believe concerning the
incomprehensible Mystery of the divine Eucharist. And as many
that say that in the book *Concerning Frequent Communion* we wrote that
it is good for Christians to receive the divine Mysteries frequently
with the proper preparation (as many Christians, that is, as are not
under a rule and do not have an impediment), with the aim of
eventually receiving the whole Christ—because, communing only
once, they do not receive His whole body—those who prattle these
things against us, I say, are the mouth of the devil, through which
the devil speaks as many things as he puts into their hearts. For we
are so far from this heretical opinion that such a thought—indeed,
even the slightest idea and suggestion of such a thing—has never

---

259 *On Matthew* 50.2, PG 58, 507; NPNF (V1-10), 302.

260 *Deprecationes* PG 96, 817A–817B; trans. *A Prayer Book for Orthodox Christians*, 351.

261 Translator's note: The *artophorion* (also known as a pyx or tabernacle) is a liturgical
vessel kept on the Holy Altar Table, in which the sanctified Gifts are stored for special
needs, such as communing the sick.

262 Cf. 1 Cor. 11:28.

entered our imagination. Wherefore we say that which was said by Susanna: "O eternal God, Who dost discern what is secret, Who art aware of all things before they come to be, Thou knowest that these men have borne false witness against us" (Sus. 42).

As an addendum we also say this: We are so opposed to the abovementioned opinions—that is, that the Mysteries are corruptible, and that the whole body of the Lord is not present in all of the parts of the sanctified bread—that, having heard that someone was planning on publishing a work containing them, we wrote to a certain sacred individual in order to prevent its publication and thus stop public prattlings and false rumors about the most-divine Mysteries, since such a work would greatly disturb the Church of Christ and mortally wound the simple brethren, who do not hold to such things. And those good brethren [our accusers], getting a hold of our letter, opened it. They opened it, read it, and adulterated it, adding to it the words, "and I say the above," in order by the addition of these words to defame us as heretics and unorthodox by the addition of these words. But may God be blessed, Who catches the wise in their deceits, according to Job.[263] For the above addition was so careless that almost all the wise teachers of the Holy Mountain saw this machination and evil creation for what it was. Wherefore, with one voice they confessed and do confess that the above phrase is an addition and an adulteration, for it has no place there syntactically according to the rules of grammar. After this misrepresentation, those grave-robbers also made copies of the adulterated document and disseminated it to many places, hoping to condemn us as heretics and to give us an evil name.

Are such things proper to Christians? Can such wickedness go any further? But would that God never reckon these things unto them. Rather, would that the Lord enlighten them and give them prudence, so that they might desist from such things and amend their ways.

As time went on, we saw and heard that many brethren were being hurt by reading this improperly opened and adulterated letter of ours. For this reason, and having been persuaded by others,

---

263 Cf. Job 5:12–13.

we went before the Common Synaxis of the Holy Mountain and petitioned for the correction of this issue. The letter mentioned below was given to us, stamped with the seal of the Community of the Holy Mountain and signed, and it was read in the famous Church of the Protaton in the hearing of all. The letter reads:

> "Most reverend Fathers and our beloved brethren in Christ living in asceticism on the Holy Mountain—in the sacred monasteries, in the sketes, and in the cells—we greet all of you with a brotherly embrace in Christ. There is nothing higher than love, and nothing sweeter than peace. For love is the sign and the distinguishing mark of the disciples of Christ, and peace is the inheritance of the Master Christ that He left to us who believe in Him, for "peace I leave with you; My peace I give to you" (Jn. 14:27). But the common enemy of the human race and originator of every evil, the devil, does not cease warring against these two chief virtues, love and peace, and those who obey his will cause hate instead of love, strife instead of peace. Why do we begin by saying these things? Because three years ago, in this place, the most wise and learned teacher Nikodemos sent a letter to a certain sacred and spiritual individual with reference to a private subject. Some perverse and warped individuals of a crooked mind took this letter into their hands while in Constantinople and opened it and read it. This is something most unlawful, something most destructive to the political society of man, and subject to the same sentence as that of grave-robbers, according to the wise Synesios.[264] And, indeed, it is condemned by the imprecations and curses of the Great Church of Christ: Wherefore a Patriarchal and Synodical Letter was issued under Patriarch Jeremiah, subjecting anyone who would open and read a foreign letter to the severest curses. So: it was not enough for those perverse individuals to merely open this letter of Nikodemos and read it, but they also

---

264 Cf. *Epistola* 142, PG 66, 1537B.

adulterated it, giving it a wrong meaning, and they copied this adulterated letter and disseminated the copies to many places on the Holy Mountain. To what end, and for what purpose? To defame the distinguished Nikodemos as a heretic and as unorthodox. Wherefore, when Nikodemos learned about these things, he came before our Common Synaxis and confessed everything that the Catholic and Eastern Church confesses, showing himself to be innocent, and not guilty of any of the accusations brought against him. And he showed that those who were defaming him were liars and slanderers. For this reason all of us, the Presidents of the twenty sacred monasteries, through our present sealed letter, notify all of the brethren living in asceticism on the Holy Mountain—in the sacred monasteries, in the sketes, and in the cells—that the aforementioned letter of Nikodemos was wrongly opened, wrongly adulterated, and wrongly misrepresented, and that copies of it were wrongly disseminated to many parts of the Holy Mountain. For such machinations and schemings are not proper to Christians, and especially to monks and preachers. From this day forth, we decree that this much-mentioned letter of Nikodemos be void and considered as invalid and nonexistent, wherever it may be found; and this applies also to its copies. And as many as have a copy of it are to burn it and not read it, nor wrongly take information from it in order to defame the aforementioned Nikodemos. For we all with one voice proclaim and confess him as most pious and most Ortho-dox, and as one nourished by the dogmas of the Church of Christ, as is evident from his sacred books which benefit all in common, in which books not a single heretical opinion is contained. And just as we confess him to be Orthodox, so should all of you come to understand this, as it is the truth. And if someone after these transpirings is provoked by that adulterated letter, and opens his mouth and speaks unjustly and slanderously against the teacher Nikodemos, he will openly be reprimanded. And he will not only be severely disciplined by our Common Synaxis, as being subject to it (being in the order and list of the Holy Mountain), but also completely exiled from this sacred place as a breeder of scandals and a lover of disturbances, and as a common enemy and corrupter of the common peace of the Holy Mountain. Everyone then must take heed to his own profession and be at peace. For, all of you being at peace with one another, the God of peace will be with you, keeping you above every encompassing circumstance. Through the intercessions of the Lady Theotokos, the especial Guardian of the Mountain, and also our Patron."

Written on July 13, in the year 1807.

+All of the Presidents
of the twenty sacred monasteries of the Holy Mountain

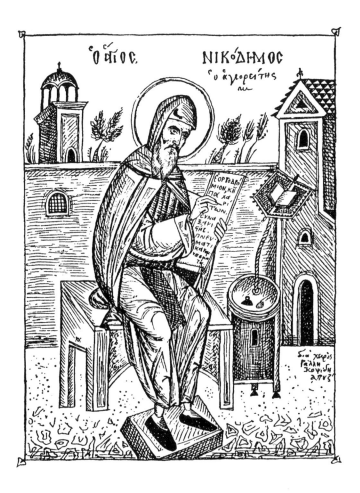

SCRIPTURAL INDEX

OLD TESTAMENT

NEW TESTAMENT

INDEX OF
SUBJECTS AND NAMES

UNCUT MOUNTAIN PRESS TITLES

Books by Archpriest Peter Heers

Fr. Peter Heers, *The Ecclesiological Renovation of Vatican II: An Orthodox Examination of Rome's Ecumenical Theology Regarding Baptism and the Church*, 2015

Fr. Peter Heers, *The Missionary Origins of Modern Ecumenism: Milestones Leading up to 1920*, 2007

The Works of our Father Among the Saints, Nikodemos the Hagiorite

Vol. 1: *Exomologetarion: A Manual of Confession*

Vol. 2: *Concerning Frequent Communion of the Immaculate Mysteries of Christ*

Vol. 3: *Confession of Faith*

Other Available Titles

Elder Cleopa of Romania, *The Truth of our Faith*

Elder Cleopa of Romania, *The Truth of our Faith, Vol. II*

Fr. John Romanides, *Patristic Theology: The University Lectures of Fr. John Romanides*

Demetrios Aslanidis and Monk Damascene Grigoriatis, *Apostle to Zaire: The Life and Legacy of Blessed Father Cosmas of Grigoriou*

Protopresbyter Anastasios Gotsopoulos, *On Common Prayer with the Heterodox According to the Canons of the Church*

Robert Spencer, *The Church and the Pope*

G. M. Davis, *Antichrist: The Fulfillment of Globalization*

Athonite Fathers of the 20th Century, Vol. I

St. Gregory Palamas, *Apodictic Treatises on the Procession of the Holy Spirit*

St. Hilarion Troitsky, *On the Dogma of the Church: An Historical Overview of the Sources of Ecclesiology*

Fr. Alexander Webster and Fr. Peter Heers, Editors, *Let No One Fear Death*

Subdeacon Nektarios Harrison, *Metropolitan Philaret of New York*

Elder George of Grigoriou, *Catholicism in the Light of Orthodoxy*

Archimandrite Ephraim Triandaphillopoulos, *Noetic Prayer as the Basis of Mission and the Struggle Against Heresy*

Dr. Nicholas Baldimtsis, *Life and Witness of St. Iakovos of Evia*

On the Reception of the Heterodox into the Orthodox Church

Select Forthcoming Titles

George, *Errors of the Latins*

Fr. Peter Heers, *Going Deeper in the Spiritual Life*

Abbe Guette, *The Papacy*

St. Hilarion Troitsky, Collected Works, Vol. II

Athonite Fathers of the 20th Century, Vol. II

This 2ⁿᵈ Edition of

CONCERNING FREQUENT COMMUNION

OF THE IMMACULATE MYSTERIES OF CHRIST

written by our Father among the Saints, Nikodemos the Hagiorite, translated by Fr. George Dokos, typeset in Baskerville, with a new cover design by George Weis in this two thousand twenty third year of our Lord's Holy Incarnation, is one of the many fine titles available from Uncut Mountain Press, translators and publishers of Orthodox Christian theological and spiritual literature. Find the book you are looking for at

uncutmountainpress.com

**GLORY BE TO GOD
FOR ALL THINGS**

AMEN.

Made in the USA
Middletown, DE
09 September 2023

37727711R00118